POPULAR
MUSIC

The Popular Music Series

Popular Music, 1920-1979 is a revised cumulation of and supersedes Volumes 1 through 8 of the *Popular Music* series, all of which are still available:

Volume 1, 2nd ed., 1950-59   Volume 5, 1920-29
Volume 2, 1940-49   Volume 6, 1965-69
Volume 3, 1960-64   Volume 7, 1970-74
Volume 4, 1930-39   Volume 8, 1975-79

This series continues with:

Volume 9, 1980-1984
Volume 10, 1985
Volume 11, 1986
Volume 12, 1987

Other Books by Bruce Pollock

In Their Own Words: Popular Songwriting, 1955-1974

The Face of Rock and Roll: Images of a Generation

When Rock Was Young: The Heyday of Top 40

When the Music Mattered: Rock in the 1960s

ISSN 0886-442X

VOLUME 12
1987

POPULAR
MUSIC

An Annotated Guide to American Popular Songs,
Including Introductory Essay, Lyricists and Composers
Index, Important Performances Index, Awards Index,
and List of Publishers

BRUCE POLLOCK
Editor

GALE RESEARCH COMPANY
BOOK TOWER ● *DETROIT, MICHIGAN 48226*

Bruce Pollock, *Editor*
Marie A. Cruz, *Editorial Assistant*

Mary Beth Trimper, *Production Manager*
Anthony J. Scolaro, *Production Assistant*
Arthur Chartow, *Art Director*

Dennis LaBeau, *Editorial Data Systems Director*
Diane H. Belickas, *Supervisor of Systems and Programming*
Theresa Rocklin, *Program Design*
Doris D. Goulart, *Editorial Data Entry Supervisor*
Jean Hinman Portfolio, *Editorial Data Entry Associate*
Joyce M. Stone, *Senior Data Entry Assistant*

Linda S. Hubbard, *Senior Editor, Popular Music Series*

Copyright © 1988 by
Gale Research Inc.

Library of Congress Catalog Card Number 85-653754
ISBN 0-8103-1810-5
ISSN 0886-442X

Computerized photocomposition by
DataServe
Bethesda, Maryland

Printed in the United States

7-12-88
recat per Joan
4-8-98 dao

Contents

About the Book and How to Use It

This volume is the twelfth of a series whose aim is to set down in permanent and practical form a selective, annotated list of the significant popular songs of our times. Other indexes of popular music have either dealt with special areas, such as jazz or theater and film music, or been concerned chiefly with songs that achieved a degree of popularity as measured by the music-business trade indicators, which vary widely in reliability.

Annual Publication Schedule

The first nine volumes in the *Popular Music* series covered sixty-five years of song history in increments of five or ten years. Volume 10 initiated a new annual publication schedule, making background information available as soon as possible after a song achieves prominence. Yearly publication also allows deeper coverage—over five hundred songs this year, instead of about three hundred, with additional details about writers' inspiration, uses of songs, album appearances, and more. (Songs with copyright dates before 1986 have full entries in this volume if not covered in the series before. Cross references lead to complete entries in earlier volumes for songs already prominent in previous years.)

Indexes Provide Additional Access

Three indexes make the valuable information in the song listings even more accessible to users. The Lyricists & Composers Index shows all the songs represented in *Popular Music,* 1987, that are credited to a given individual. The Important Performances Index (introduced in the revised cumulation, *Popular Music, 1920-1979)* tells at a glance what albums, musicals, films, television shows, or other media featured songs that are represented in the volume. The "Vocalist" category—first added to the index in the 1986 volume—allows the user to see with what songs an artist has been associated this year. The index is arranged by broad media category, then alphabetically by the show or album title, with the songs listed under each title. Finally, the Awards Index (also introduced in the cumulation) provides a list of the songs nominated for awards by the American Academy of Motion Picture Arts and Sciences (Academy Award), the American Academy of Recording Arts and Sciences (Grammy Award), and the Country Music Association. Winning songs are indicated by asterisks.

List of Publishers

The List of Publishers is an alphabetically arranged directory providing addresses for the publishers of the songs represented in this twelfth volume of *Popular Music*. Also noted is the organization handling performance rights for the publisher—American Society of Composers, Authors, and Publishers (ASCAP)... Broadcast Music, Inc. (BMI) ... or Society of European Stage Authors and Composers (SESAC).

Tracking Down Information on Songs

Unfortunately, the basic records kept by the active participants in the music business are often casual, inaccurate, and transitory. There is no single source of comprehensive information about popular songs, and those sources that do exist do not publish complete material about even the musical works with which they are directly concerned. Two of the primary proprietors of basic information about our popular music are the major performing rights societies—ASCAP and BMI. Although each of these organizations has considerable information about the songs of its own writer and publisher members and has also issued indexes of its own songs, their files and published indexes are designed primarily for clearance identification by the commercial users of music. Their publications of annual or periodic lists of their "hits" necessarily include only a small fraction of their songs, and the facts given about these are also limited. Both ASCAP and BMI are, however, invaluable and indispensable sources of data about popular music. It is just that their data and special knowledge are not readily accessible to the researcher.

Another basic source of information about musical compositions and their creators and publishers is the Copyright Office of the Library of Congress. There a computerized file lists each published, unpublished, republished, and renewed copyright of songs registered with the Office since 1979. This is helpful for determining the precise date of the declaration of the original ownership of musical works, but contains no other information. To complicate matters further, some authors, composers, and publishers have been known to employ rather makeshift methods of protecting their works legally, and there are songs listed in *Popular Music* that may not be found in the Library of Congress files.

Selection Criteria

In preparing this series, the editor was faced with a number of separate problems. The first and most important of these was that of selection. The stated aim of the project—to offer the user as comprehensive and accurate a listing of significant popular songs as possible—has been the guiding criterion. The purpose has never been to offer a judgment on the quality of any songs or to indulge a prejudice for or against any type of popular music. Rather, it is the purpose of *Popular Music* to document those musical works that (1) achieved a substantial degree of popular acceptance, (2) were exposed to the public in especially notable circumstances, or (3) were accepted and given important performances by influential musical and dramatic artists.

Another problem was whether or not to classify the songs as to type. Most works of music are subject to any number of interpretations and, although it is possible to describe a particular performance, it is more difficult to give a musical composition a label applicable not only to its origin but to its subsequent musical history. In fact, the most significant versions of some songs are often quite at variance with their origins. Citations for such songs in *Popular Music* indicate the important facts about not only their origins but also their subsequent lives, rather than assigning an arbitrary and possibly misleading label.

Research Sources

The principal sources of information for the titles, authors, composers, publishers, and dates of copyright of the songs in this volume were the Copyright Office of the Library of Congress, ASCAP, BMI, and individual writers and publishers. Data about best-selling recordings were obtained principally from two of the leading music business trade journals—*Billboard* and *Cash Box*. For the historical notes; information about foreign, folk, public domain, and classical origins; and identification of theatrical, film, and television introducers of songs, the editor relied upon collections of record album notes, theater programs, sheet music, newspaper and magazine articles, and other material, both his own and that in the Lincoln Center Library for the Performing Arts in New York City.

Contents of a Typical Entry

The primary listing for a song includes

- Title and alternate title(s)
- Country of origin (for non-U.S. songs)
- Author(s) and composer(s)

9

- Current publisher, copyright date
- Annotation on the song's origins or performance history

Title: The full title and alternate title or titles are given exactly as they appear on the Library of Congress copyright record or, in some cases, the sheet music. Since even a casual perusal of the book reveals considerable variation in spelling and punctuation, it should be noted that these are neither editorial nor typographical errors but the colloquialisms of the music trade. The title of a given song as it appears in this series is, in almost all instances, the one under which it is legally registered.

Foreign Origin: If the song is of foreign origin, the primary listing indicates the country of origin after the title. Additional information may be noted, such as the original title, copyright date, writer, publisher in country of origin, or other facts about the adaptation.

Authorship: In all cases, the primary listing reports the author or authors and the composer or composers. The reader may find variations in the spelling of a songwriter's name. This results from the fact that some writers used different forms of their names at different times or in connection with different songs. These variants appear in the Lyricists & Composers Index as well. In addition to this kind of variation in the spelling of writers' names, the reader will also notice that in some cases, where the writer is also the performer, the name as a writer may differ from the form of the name used as a performer.

Publisher: The current publisher is listed. Since *Popular Music* is designed as a practical reference work rather than an academic study, and since copyrights more than occasionally change hands, the current publisher is given instead of the original holder of the copyright. If a publisher has, for some reason, copyrighted a song more than once, the years of the significant copyright subsequent to the year of the original copyright are also listed after the publisher's name.

Annotation: The primary listing mentions significant details about the song's history—the musical, film, or other production in which the song was introduced or featured and, where important, by whom it was introduced, in the case of theater and film songs . . . any other performers identified with the song . . . first or best-selling recordings and album inclusions, indicating the performer and the record company . . . awards . . . and other relevant data. The name of a performer may be listed differently in connection with different songs, especially over a period of years. The name listed is the form of the name given in connection with a particular performance or record. It should be noted that the designation "best-selling record" does not mean that the record was a "hit." It means simply that the record or records noted as "best-selling" were the best-selling record or records of that particular song, in comparison with the sales of other records of the same song. Dates are provided for important recordings and performances.

Cross-References

Any alternate titles appearing in bold type after the main title in a primary listing are also cross-referenced in the song listings. If a song previously covered in the *Popular Music* series also attained prominence in 1986, the title and new achievement are noted here with a reference to the appropriate earlier volume.

Popular Music in 1987

Extending and deepening the forms and content that made the 1985-1986 period of songwriting so exhilarating, 1987 offered little that was downright daring or outright revolutionary, yet it extended this particular song heyday another year through its diversity and overall strength. If nothing took over the year the way patriotic pride and the threat of censorship did 1985 or the sudden unilateral maturation of pop did 1986, this year at least enlarged upon the prevailing themes with grace and taste. With the wheel already re-invented, all-weather radials were now affixed to some fine motor vehicles. And while in good creative weather like this there could be no real losers (unlike the late 1970's, when disco reigned, or the early 1980's, when MTV called the tune), some definite winners did emerge in this year of steady, unspectacular growth.

Broadway, long as dormant an urban landscape as country music has been a rural one, suddenly found itself turning green as Spring and green as money, sprouting tendrils called *Starlight Express, Les Miserables,* and *Phantom of the Opera,* which in turn sprouted long lines at the ticket window and much optimism for the future. At the same time, after 1986, when the average age of the pop song purveyor seemed as if it must have been thirty-five plus, the under twenty-one (in many cases the under eighteen) crowd made bold moves to reclaim some emotional turf with the drive and energy for which the teen age is known. These elements were previously weak links in the creative chain, but abundance stretched across 1987 in a nearly unbroken horizon of songwriting excellence.

Remakes and Comebacks

It is ironic, however, in a year when the raucous sounds of adolescent rebellion dominated the radio waves—from the abject defiance of "You Gotta Fight for Your Right to Party" and the blatant sexism of "Girls, Girls, Girls" and "Talk Dirty to Me," to the more uplifting yet no less threatening sentiments contained in "Wanted Dead or Alive" and "The Final Countdown"—that by far the year's most interesting develop-ment was the preponderance of remakes from the fifties and early sixties. Never an entirely moribund genre, in 1987 revivals proved a remarkably fecund resource; and the amazing number of artists on the comeback trail, with weathered voices fully restored, offered implicit and explicit messages of renewal and hope intact.

For the most part these artists attached the accrued goodwill of their previous images to current works of sophisticated and pointed content. Robbie Robertson ("Sweet Fire of Love"), the Grateful Dead ("Touch of Grey"), Elton John ("Candle in the Wind"), Cher ("I Found Someone"), Stevie Wonder ("Skeletons"), Fleetwood Mac ("Seven Wonders"), and George Harrison ("When We Was Fab") found the atmosphere quite receptive to their newly-minted personas, often nothing more than last year's model with a spiffy paint job, or, in the case of the Grateful Dead, a dab of Grecian Formula. Robbie Robertson's work was perhaps the most advanced and eloquent of the comeback pack, revealing with songs like "Sonny Got Caught in the Moonlight" and "Fallen Angel" a sure poetic voice even stronger than his earthy odes as a member of the Band. And Cher's comeback was certainly a multi-media event, including, besides an album, twin bravura performances in the films *Suspect* and *Moonstruck* that once again reclaimed for her the inside track position as the generation's hippest natural.

Other comebacks now in the 1987 record books included those by Natalie Cole ("Jump Start"), Brian Wilson ("Let's Go to Heaven in My Car"), Pink Floyd ("Learning to Fly"), Roger Waters ("Radio Waves"), Aerosmith ("Dude Looks Like a Lady"), Squeeze ("Hourglass"), Richard Carpenter ("Something in Your Eyes"), and the Pet Shop Boys ("What Have I Done to Deserve This"); the latter two recordings were enhanced by the voice of Dusty Springfield, who was herself making a comeback. Of course, there was also the highly touted return of Michael Jackson, whose previous album, *Thriller,* was merely the biggest seller of all time. Despite predictable hits from the new release ("The Way You Make Me Feel," "Bad," "I Can't Stop Loving You"), the overwhelming critical reaction was disappointment. Maybe it was simply that *Bad* was no *Thriller,* or that Jackson should have taken the rest of the decade off before coming back. In any case, with these and other familiar faces and voices all clattering and colliding on radio and television screens, listeners were treated to thirty years of pop music history nearly every time they switched on the dial.

And if the performer of preference wasn't at the moment available, you could always count on a contemporary remake of one of their classic oldies to fill the bill. Like standards from pop's most pre-eminent era, the thirties and forties, rock songs from the fifties and sixties became the chestnuts of 1987, whose viability in a multitude of cross-media formats assured them a life well beyond the limits heretofore assumed. Thus, television's zany kids' show host PeeWee Herman sang "Surfin' Bird" in an Annette Funicello/Frankie Avalon nostalgia flick, *Return to the Beach,* and the animated pitchmen California Raisins reprised their television commercial remake of "I Heard It Through the Grapevine," surely one of the more convoluted journeys back to the hitsville of any title in song history (the popular country song "Hymne," formerly a wine commercial, pales in comparison, as does the ride Genesis took to the top of the charts on "Tonight, Tonight, Tonight," courtesy of its incessant use as a beer commercial).

On the other side of the coin of commerce, much controversy was caused by the use of the Beatles' "Revolution" to sell running shoes, while George Harrison's "Something in the Way She Moves" was hardly noticed as an aid to moving cars. We had rock ballads turned into country songs in three-part harmony ("To Know Him Is to Love Him," as sung by the trio of Linda Ronstadt, Dolly Parton, and Emmylou Harris); we had classic neo-rhythm 'n' blues turned into moviestar camp ("Little Darlin' " as sung by Warren Beatty and Dustin Hoffman in the box office disaster *Ishtar*). Also in 1987 we had a pop chanteuse who remade one of her own hits from the sixties ("As Tears Go By," by Marianne Faithfull) and a modern vintage singer who remade a tune that had already been remade a couple of other times and, like her predecessors, saw it reach number one (Kim Wilde, whose version of "You Keep Me Hanging On" joined the original by the Supremes and the later edition by the Vanilla Fudge as chart-toppers). The otherwise obscure sixties songwriter Denny Cordell experienced a rare daily double when two of his tunes were revived and shared the same top ten ("I Think We're Alone Now," and "Mony Mony"). Finally, we had an obscure flipside of a fifties top ten single not only become a number one song itself, but serve as the title to the hit movie that launched its revival ("La Bamba").

New Songwriters Emerge

Yet with all this seemingly regressive activity, by far the strongest mark on the landscape of 1987 was made by the new generation of songwriting voices asserting themselves with uncommon individuality. While songwriting outfits like U2 ("With or Without You," "I Still Haven't Found What I'm Looking For"), REM ("The One I Love," "It's the End of the World As We Know It and I Feel Fine"), and Los Lobos ("The Hardest Time," "One Time One Night") had all produced quality works before, this was a year that found them all breaking through to new levels of popular awareness, an accomplishment made all the more admirable by the lack of commercial compromise on the part of any of these groups. Meanwhile, pushing the creative envelope even wider, new artists in bands named Firetown, 10,000 Maniacs, Crowded House, and Camper Van Beethoven more than kept the promise implicit in the works of their brethren and forbears, with songs like "Verdi Cried," "Heart Country," "Don't Dream It's Over," and "Joe Stalin's Cadillac," respectively. Add Julie Brown's properly dyspeptic "The Homecoming Queen's Got a Gun," Andy White's Dylanesque "Reality Row," and Mojo Nixon's antic "Elvis Is Everywhere" and you might have the groundwork for the first wave of remakes of the year 2007.

In 1987 even the established songwriters of the day were stretching toward new plateaus of experience. Bruce Springsteen, known for his boyish boardwalk bravado, turned "The Tunnel of Love" into his own harrowing metaphor of the marital state. Mose Allison, long a droll treasurehouse of emotional information, had a different perspective on the situation in "Puttin' up with Me," while John Hiatt, coming closer to his own in 1987, nailed the issue shut with "Learning How to Love You." If Loudon Wainwright in "I Eat Out" and Prince in "Housequake" were content to explore familiar quirky terrain, John Cougar Mellencamp was not afraid to reveal a sentimental side in "Cherry Bomb." Julie Gold wrote one of country music's finest songs of the year, "From a Distance," for Nanci Griffith, who wrote another, "Beacon Street," for herself. And when writers weren't reaching inside for material, they were drawing material from some of the year's biggest events and issues.

Headlines into Songs

Surely 1987 will be thought of as the year in which children in jeopardy kept us in almost constant turmoil, from the girl in the well in Texas to the one who survived the airline crash in Detroit to the one who didn't survive the beatings of her parents in New York City. Songwriters took appropriate note: Suzanne Vega's "Luka," Natalie Merchant's "What's the Matter Here," and "Dear Mr. Jesus" by Powersource all gave trenchant musical voice to the subject of child abuse. The AIDS epidemic prompted a re-examination of attitudes on sexuality that ad hoc censorship groups could never attain. As usual, rap groups, the cutting edge urban troubadours, delivered the message at its most basic level in songs like "Go See the Doctor," by Kool Moe Dee, written during a visit to a walk-in clinic, and "Protect Yourself," by the Fat Boys, which debuted on the television sex discussion show hosted by Dr. Ruth Westheimer. Even in country music, as far from rap as north is from the south, precautions were the rule, as epitomized by "I Want to Know You Before We Make Love," the hit for Conway Twitty. But since the sex drive is what causes popular music's turntable to turn, there were those who instinctively resisted even the most eminently plausible admonishments. In 1987 they paid a stiff price. George Michael's "I Want Your Sex" was widely regarded as irresponsible (it hit the top of the charts anyway); "Walk with an Erection," a parody of 1986's "Walk Like an Egyptian," so outraged the original copyright owners that permission to record it was denied (it was released anyway); and Luther Campbell's rather blatant "We Want Some Pussy" resulted in the arrest of a record store clerk merely for ringing up its sale (she was later cleared of the charges). On a lesser though no less dramatic moral scale, songs of the religious experience made news, ranging from Andy Partridge's existential atheism in "Dear God," to Tammy Faye Bakker's essential egotism in "The Ballad of Jim and Tammy," alluding, of course, to the precipitous fall of the Bakkers' television ministry, a subject the Hooters addressed in "Satellite" and Ray Stevens convincingly questioned in "Would Jesus Wear a Rolex." Only Stevie Nicks' heartfelt remake of "Silent Night" seemed to restore the lustre of traditional religion.

Some of the year's best songs were of the sort that might have been termed to protest music back in the early sixties. In 1987 they were pop songs: Sting's eerie "They Dance Alone," U2's chilling "Where the Streets Have No Name," Timbuk 3's "All I Want for Christmas," a pointed anti-war toys lament, Steven Van Zandt's raucous "Trail of Broken Treaties," and the moving re-release of "Biko," the song penned by Peter Gabriel that inspired the 1987 movie *Cry Freedom*.

Film Music

With soundtrack albums complete with anthemic closing rock finales now as obligatory and entrenched a moviegoer item as popcorn, once again in the battle of the screens the silver easily outdid the tube as haven for both abject filler and the unearthed gem. That few connoisseurs otherwise would have heard Neil Young's "We've Never Danced," but for Martha Davis's version on the soundtrack album of *Made in Heaven* may seem argument enough for those devoted to the genre. Far more in the majority were the viewers of films like *Dirty Dancing* and *Beverly Hills Cop 2,* who composed a good deal of the listening crowd that made "I've Had the Time of My Life," and "She's Like the Wind," from the former, and "Shakedown" and "Cross My Broken Heart," from the latter into some of the year's biggest sellers. With success like that, who needed musicals?

17

Songs from the Theater

Broadway did. If in the past two seasons you could count on the fingers of one mitten the number of original Broadway musical mega-hits, 1987 made up not only for the years past, but gave promise, at least in several theaters, of filling seats throughout the remainder of the decade. The man most responsible for this revival was the English composer Andrew Lloyd Webber, whose *Evita, Cats,* and *Jesus Christ, Superstar,* had done much to keep the musical alive, if barely breathing, for the past decade. In 1987 he brought forth *Starlight Express* and *Phantom of the Opera,* both road tested in England and chart-tested with singles and LP packages. *Starlight*'s album consisted of modern popstars not associated with the show offering interpretations of its tunes ("Only You," "I Am the Starlight"); the cast album of *Phantom* produced several large hits in England, among them "Music of the Night" and "All I Ask of You." These recordings provided readymade audiences for each show's opening night. (*Phantom* did not officially open until early in 1988, but tickets had been selling for most of the preceding year.) Another hugely successful epic imported from abroad was *Les Miserables,* eventually sporting both an American and an English cast album for its memorable songs, including "On My Own" and "I Dreamed a Dream." On top of that, our own Stephen Sondheim was back on the boards with another of his complex, metaphorical tales, *Into the Woods,* from which the title tune and "Agony" deserve special mention.

In addition to the obvious winners of the season, some promising names either arrived on the scene (Douglas J. Cohen with *No Way to Treat a Lady*) or continued compiling credentials for a major breakthrough (Craig Carnelia once again garnered fine notices for "She Was K.C. at Seven," from *3 Postcards,* and "Privacy," from the much-heralded *No Frills Revue.*) And at year's end John Kander and Fred Ebb revived their *Flora, the Red Menace* with previously unheard material like "The Kid Herself." In all this, the fact that the Tim Rice opus *Chess* would at last be opening in 1988, seemed to lose a lot of its once game-saving significance.

Country and Folk Music

Nashville, however, could have used a home run in 1987. The much-heralded 1986 infusion of new blood down those old mill streams, with fully developed young superstars like Dwight Yoakum, Steve Earle, Holly Dunn, Lyle Lovett, Nanci Griffith, and Randy Travis taking center stage, proved primarily an interesting ruse designed to provide new outlets for the same established songwriting teams. Works by Paul Overstreet and Don Schlitz ("Forever and Ever Amen"), Sonny LeMaire and J. P. Pennington ("She's Too Good to Be True"), and others, while as polished as anything either the left coast or the right might have produced, hardly qualified as a revolution or anything more than a two-base hit. More interesting was the line many of the best country performers were crossing into folk music, a territory where expression might be just a bit freer. Lyle Lovett ("God Will") and Nanci Griffith ("Ford Econoline," "There's a Light Beyond These Woods, Mary Margaret") traversed those borders with ease. John Prine crossed from folk to country with "Let's Talk Dirty in Hawaiian" and "Out of Love." Wendy Waldman came to Nashville via Los Angeles with her work on "Fishing in the Dark"; Ian Tyson came down from Canada with some excellent tunes ("Summer Wages," "Navajo Rug"); country/ folk living legend Townes Van Zandt provided inspiration with "For the Sake of the Song." The English folk troupe Fairport Convention reconvened with "Close to the Wind" and Richard Thompson's revived "Meet on the Ledge." Slightly more sophisticated tastes could find all the sustenance they needed in songs by Loudon Wainwright ("Hard Day on the Planet," "The Back Nine") and Christine Lavin ("Another Woman's Man"). Richie Havens, a major folk voice of the sixties, was briefly given a reprieve from singing commercials and put back behind some quality material like John Martyn's "I Don't Wanna Know" and his own "Simple Things."

Rhythm 'n' Blues

In 1987 the world of rhythm 'n' blues was far from simple. From the streets to the penthouses, careers tumbled and shook with the seismic intensity of a typical week in Los Angeles. If Michael Jackson's new album was tainted with a bit too much of his semi-private persona, Whitney Houston, having none, was able to survive similar lackluster notices, largely through the strength of ballads by some of pop song's reigning royalty: Michael Masser and Will Jennings ("Didn't We Almost Have It All") and Billy Steinberg and Tom Kelly ("So Emotional"). Last year's songwriting princes, Jimmy Jam and Terry Lewis, could only muster "Fake" for their 1987 resume, while Prince himself rebounded from his disastrous movie, *Under the Cherry Moon,* with surprisingly good reviews for his autobiographical documentary, *Sign o' of the Times,* especially for its music —"U Got the Look," "I Could Never Take the Place of Your Man." While the soul queens Aretha Franklin and Natalie Cole were both on the scene making interesting noises this year, new pretenders to their throne emerged in the persons of Lisa Lisa ("Lost in Emotion") and Jody Watley

("Looking for a New Love," "Still a Thrill"). Smokey Robinson made a comeback in 1987 ("Just to See Her"), but the crooning turf was in no danger of being swiped from Freddie Jackson ("Jam Tonight," "I Don't Want to Lose Your Love").

By far the most pleasing development to cross from the rhythm 'n' blues sanctuary into the wider world was the emergence of Robert Cray. With "Smoking Gun" and "Right Next Door Because of Me," Cray brought a taste of the blues back not only to rhythm 'n' blues and to the radio waves, but to the arena concert stages of America and subsequently to the upper quarter of the charts, with the ghosts of Muddy Waters and Robert Johnson, Son House and Lightning Hopkins nodding in the wings. In a world where a bluesman, even one as slick and refined as Cray, can reign as king of the hill, even for a little while, anything is possible.

POPULAR
MUSIC

A

(You're Puttin') A Rush on Me
Words and music by Timmy Allen and Paul Lawrence.
Willesden Music, Inc., 1987/Bush Burnin' Music.
Best-selling record by Stephanie Mills, from the album *If I Were Your Woman* (MCA, 87).

Agony
Words and music by Stephen Sondheim.
Revelation Music Publishing Corp., 1986/Rilting Music Inc.
Introduced by Chuck Wagner and Robert Westenberg in the Stephen Sondheim musical *Into the Woods,* which opened on Broadway in 1987.

Ain't No Cure for Love (Canadian)
Words and music by Leonard Cohen.
Stranger Music Inc., 1986.
Performed by Jennifer Warnes on the album *Famous Blue Raincoat,* (Cypress, 86), a collection of works written by the gifted Canadian songwriter-novelist-poet, Leonard Cohen, who also wrote the book *Beautiful Losers* and the popular ballad "Suzanne" (for which, see *Popular Music, 1920-1979*).

All I Ask of You (English)
Words by Charles Hart, music by Andrew Lloyd Webber.
The Really Useful Group, England, 1987.
Introduced by Sarah Brightman in the London production of the musical *The Phantom of the Opera,* which opened on Broadway early in 1988. Performed on the cast album by Steve Barton; the song reached the top ten in England.

All I Want for Christmas
Words and music by Pat MacDonald.
Mambadaddi, 1987/I.R.S.
Introduced by Timbuk 3 (I.R.S., 87). Proceeds from this protest

against war toys were donated to the campaign to eliminate such toys.

All My Ex's Live in Texas
Words and music by Sanger D. Shafer and Lyndia J. Shafer.
Acuff Rose Opryland, 1986.
Best-selling record in 1987 by George Strait, from the album *Ocean Front Property* (MCA, 86). Nominated for a Grammy Award, Country Song of the Year, 1987.

Alone
Words and music by Billy Steinberg and Tom Kelly.
Billy Steinberg Music, 1987/Denise Barry Music.
Best-selling record by Heart from the album *Bad Animals* (Capitol, 87). Introduced by the authors on an obscure album called *1-10.* After a rewrite, it was shown to Heart, who brought it to number one.

Always
Words and music by Jonathan Lewis, David Lewis, and Wayne Lewis.
Jodaway Music, 1987.
Best-selling record by Atlantic Starr, from the album *All in the Name of Love* (Warner Bros., 87). This ballad has become an instant wedding classic.

Always the Sun (English)
Words and music by The Stranglers.
Plumbshaft Ltd., 1987/CBS Songs Ltd.
Best-selling record by the Stranglers, from their album *Dreamtime* (Columbia, 87); this song has proved one of the more accessible efforts from the well known British post-punk turned-art-rock ensemble.

Am I Blue
Revived by George Strait on the album *Ocean Front Property* (MCA). See *Popular Music, 1920-1979.*

American Me (English)
Words and music by Thom Schuyler and Fred Knobloch.
A La Mode Music, 1987/Uncle Artie/Writer's Group Music/ Lawyer's Daughter.
Introduced by Schuyler, Knobloch & Overstreet, from their album *SKO* (MTM, 87). The song was later customized by the authors for the use of 24 major league and 17 minor league baseball teams.

Angel
Words and music by Angela Winbush.
Dead or Alive Music Ltd., England, 1987.
Introduced by Angela Winbush on her album *Sharp* (Mercury, 87),
which was the rhythm 'n' blues songwriter's first solo effort. She
previously recorded as a member of Rene and Angela.

Angelyne
Words and music by Bruce Springsteen.
Bruce Springsteen Publishing, 1986.
Performed by the Nitty Gritty Dirt Band on the album *Hold On*
(Warner Bros., 86). With this song author Springsteen's reach
extended into the country-pop realm.

Animal (English)
Words and music by Steve Clark, Phil Collen, Mutt Lange, and
Rick Savage.
Calloco, 1987/Zomba Enterprises, Inc.
Best-selling record by Def Leppard, the British heavy metal group,
from their album *Hysteria* (Mercury, 87).

Another Woman's Man
Words and music by Christine Lavin.
Flip a Jig, 1987/Rounder.
Performed by Christine Lavin on her album *Another Woman's Man*
(Philo, 87), this song formed part of a treatise on modern marri-
age and divorce.

Another World
Words and music by John Leffler and Ralph Schuckett.
Fountain Square Music Publishing Co. Inc, 1987.
Best-selling record by Crystal Gayle and Gary Morris. Introduced
as the theme for the TV series *Another World.* Recorded by Gayle
on her album *What If We Fall in Love* (Warner Bros., 87).

Anyone Who Had a Heart
Revived by Luther Vandross on his album *Give Me the Reason*
(Epic, 86). See *Popular Music 1920-1979.*

As Tears Go By (English)
Revived in 1987 by Marianne Faithfull on her album *Strange
Weather* (EMI, 87); the same artist had used the song to launch
her career in 1964, when Mick Jagger wrote it for her. See *Popular
Music, 1920-1979.*

B

Baby's Got a Hold on Me
Words and music by Josh Leo, Jeff Hanna, and Bob Carpenter.
Warner-Elektra-Asylum Music Inc., 1986/Mopage/Warner-Refuge
  Music Inc./Moolagenous.
Best-selling record by the Nitty Gritty Dirt Band, from their album
  Hold On (Warner Bros., 86).

Baby's Got a New Baby
Words and music by J. Fred Knobloch and Dan Tyler.
A Little More Music Inc., 1987/Sharp Circle/Uncle Artie.
Best-selling record by Schuyler, Knobloch & Overstreet, from their
  album *SKO* (MTM, 87).

Back and Forth
Words and music by Kevin Kendricks, Tomi Jenkins, Nathan
  Leftenant, and Larry Blackmon.
All Seeing Eye Music, 1986/Polygram Music Publishing Inc./Better
  Days Music/Polygram Songs.
Best-selling record by Cameo, from the album *Word Up* (Atlanta
  Artists, 86).

Back in Baby's Arms
Words and music by Bob Montgomery.
Talmont Music Co., 1987.
Introduced by Emmylou Harris on the soundtrack of the 1987 film
  Planes, Trains, and Automobiles; released on the soundtrack
  album (Hughes/MCA, 87).

Back in the High Life Again
Words by Will Jennings, music by Steve Winwood.
F.S. Ltd., England, 1986/Willin' David/Blue Sky Rider Songs.
Best-selling record by Steve Winwood, from his album *Back in the
  High Life* (Island, 86). Nominated for a Grammy Award,
  Record of the Year, 1987.

The Back Nine
Words and music by Loudon Wainwright.
Snowden Music, 1986.
Introduced by Loudon Wainright, from the album *More Love Songs* (Rounder, 87); marks a return to form by the noted, autobiographically inclined folk balladeer, in which he likens his life to a game of golf.

Back to Paradise
Words and music by Giraldo, Jim Vallance, and Bryan Adams.
Calypso Toonz, 1987/Irving Music Inc./Big Tooth Music Corp./ Rare Blue Music, Inc./TCF.
Best-selling record by 38 Special, from the movie *Revenge of the Nerds* (87); also released on the soundtrack album (A & M, 87).

Bad
Words and music by Michael Jackson.
Mijac Music, 1987/Warner-Tamerlane Publishing Corp.
Best-selling record by Michael Jackson, from his album of the same title (Epic, 87); this was a long-awaited follow-up to the record-breaking success of Jackson's *Thriller.*

Bad Influence
Words and music by Robert Cray and Mike Vannice.
Calhoun Street, 1983.
Introduced by Eric Clapton on his album *August* (Duck, 86). Noted blues singer-guitarist Clapton significantly aided the career of author Cray, also a blues artist, when he took up this song.

The Ballad of Jim and Tammy
Words by Tammy Faye Bakker, music by Tom T. Hall.
Unichappell Music Inc., 1987.
Introduced by Tammy Faye Bakker (Sutra, 87). By re-using the music to "Harper Valley PTA" (see *Popular Music, 1920-1979*), Bakker offered her side of the scandal that ousted herself and her husband from their evangelical empire.

Ballerina Girl
Words and music by Lionel Richie.
Brockman Enterprises Inc., 1986.
Best-selling record by Lionel Richie, from his album *Dancing on the Ceiling* (Motown, 86).

Battle Lines
Words by Hal Hackaday, music by Richard Kapp.
Introduced by Beth Fowler in the 1987 musical *Teddy and Alice.* All

of the songs in this musical were adapted from marches by John Philip Sousa.

Battleship Chains
Words and music by Terry Anderson.
Tomato du Plenti, 1986.
Best-selling record by the Georgia Satellites, from their album of the same name (Elektra, 86). The author is a member of NRBQ, often fondly referred to as "America's bar band."

Be There
Words and music by Allee Willis and Franne Golde.
Ensign Music Corp., 1987/Off Backstreet Music/Franne Gee/ Rightsong Music Inc.
Best-selling record by the Pointer Sisters, from the film and soundtrack album *Beverly Hills Cop II* (MCA, 87).

Beacon Street
Words and music by Nanci Griffith.
Wing & Wheel, 1987.
Introduced by Nanci Griffith, from the album *Lone Star State of Mind* (MCA, 87).

Big Love
Words and music by Lindsay Buckingham.
Now Sounds Music, 1987.
Best-selling record by Fleetwood Mac, from the album *Tango in the Night* (Warner Bros., 87). Soon after album's release, Buckingham left the band to resume his solo career.

Big Time (English)
Words and music by Peter Gabriel.
Cliofine, England, 1986/Hidden Pun.
Best-selling record by Peter Gabriel, from the album *So* (Geffen, 86). The artist and album were voted best of the year in many annual polls, including that in *Rolling Stone* magazine.

Biko (English)
Words and music by Peter Gabriel.
Hidden Pun, 1983.
 Revived in 1987 by Joan Baez on her album *Recently* (Gold Castle). The noted folksinger and activist of the 1960's chose this song about the South African black leader murdered in 1977 to initiate her comeback. Composer Gabriel also re-released his own rendition (Geffen, 87), proceeds from which went to the International Defense and Aid Fund for South Africa and to the Africa Fund. Biko was also the subject of the film *Cry Freedom,* released in 1987.

Bitter Fruit
Words and music by Steve Van Zant.
Little Steven Music, 1987.
Introduced by Little Steven on his album *Freedom--No Compromise* (Manhattan, 87), with guest vocalist Ruben Blades. This song, dedicated to the plight of migrant workers, highlighted the album of neo-protest music by the former guitarist in Bruce Springsteen's E Street Band.

Blue Hotel
Words and music by Chris Isaak.
Chris Isaak Music Publishing, 1987.
Introduced by Chris Isaak on his album, also called *Chris Isaak* (Warner Bros., 87). This was one of six Isaak cuts showcased on the television series *Private Eye;* the rockabilly sound of his material suited the atmosphere of this detective show set in Los Angeles in the 1950's.

Bonnie Jean (Little Sister)
Words and music by David Lynn Jones.
Mighty Nice Music, 1983/Hat Band Music.
Introduced by David Lynn Jones on the album *Hard Times on Easy Street* (Mercury, 87).

Born to Be Wild
Revived in 1987 by the Cult, from the album *Electric* (Electric). Following the success of their revival, the songwriter, John Kay, released a comeback album of old material. See *Popular Music, 1920-1979.*

Born to Boogie
Words and music by Hank Williams, Jr.
Bocephus Music Inc., 1987.
Best-selling record by Hank Williams, Jr., from the album of the same title (Warner/Curb, 87).

Boys Night Out
Words and music by Timothy B. Schmidt, Will Jennings, and Bruce Gaitsch.
Jeddrah Music, 1987/Blue Sky Rider Songs/Willin' David/Edge of Fluke.
Best-selling record by Timothy B. Schmidt, from the album *Timothy B.* (MCA, 87), marking a return by a former member of the Eagles.

Brand New Lover (English)
Words and music by Peter Burns, Michael Percy, Timothy Lever,

and Steven Coy.
Dead or Alive Music Ltd., England, 1986/WB Music Corp.
Best-selling record by Dead or Alive, from the album *Mad, Bad, and Dangerous to Know* (Epic, 86).

Breakout (English)
Words and music by Swing Out Sister.
Virgin Nymph, 1987.
Best-selling record by Swing Out Sister, from the album *It's Better to Travel* (Mercury, 87).

Breath Away from Heaven
Words and music by George Harrison.
Ganga Publishing Co., 1987/Zero Productions.
Introduced by George Harrison on the soundtrack of the film *Shanghai Surprise,* which was financed by ex-Beatle Harrison. He also performed the song on his album *Cloud Nine* (Dark Horse, 87).

Brilliant Disguise
Words and music by Bruce Springsteen.
Bruce Springsteen Publishing, 1987.
Best-selling record by Bruce Springsteen, from the album *Tunnel of Love* (Columbia, 87). This low-key release, Springsteen's first since his hugely successful *Born in the USA* album, also made the top ten.

The Broken Pianolita (Brazilian)
English words by Robert Wright and George Forrest, music by Heitor Villa-Lobos.
Revived by John Raitt in the 1987 production of the operetta *Magdelena,* staged in New York City to celebrate the one-hundredth anniversary of composer Villa Lobos's birth. Raitt was in the original 1948 production as well, which closed after 88 performances because of a musicians' strike. This song was dropped after opening night, however. The lyricists also collaborated on "Stranger in Paradise," among others.

Burning Love
Introduced by Elvis Presley, this song was revived in 1987 by Doctor and the Medics on the album *Burning Love* (IRS). See *Popular Music, 1920-1979.*

C

Can I Let Her Go
Words by Hal Hackaday, music by Richard Kapp.
Introduced by Len Cariou in the 1987 musical *Teddy and Alice*.
  This ballad was adapted from "The March of the Thunderer" by
  John Philip Sousa.

Candle in the Wind (English)
Words by Bernie Taupin, music by Elton John.
Dick James Music Inc., 1973/Polygram Music Publishing Inc.
Revived in 1987 by Elton John on his album *Live in Australia with
  the Melbourne Symphony Orchestra* (MCA). He had originally
  recorded the song, which was inspired by the life and death of
  Marilyn Monroe, in 1973 on *Yellow Brick Road*.

Candy
Words and music by Larry Blackmon and Tomi Jenkins.
All Seeing Eye Music, 1987/Polygram Music Publishing Inc./Better
  Days Music/Polygram Songs.
Best-selling record by Cameo, from the album *Word Up* (Polygram,
  86).

Can't Hardly Wait
Words and music by Paul Westerberg.
NAH Music, 1987.
Introduced by the Replacements, from the album *Pleased to Meet
  Me* (Sire, 87).

Can't Stop My Heart from Loving You
Words and music by Jamie O'Hara and Kieran Kane.
Cross Keys Publishing Co., Inc., 1987/Tree Publishing Co., Inc./
  Kieran Kane.
Best-selling record by the O'Kanes, from the album *The O'Kanes*
  (Columbia, 87).

Can't We Try (Canadian)
Words and music by Dan Hill and B. Hill.
Cak Songs, 1987/Songs of Jennifer/If Dreams Had Wings/A Question of Material/Scoop.
Best-selling record by Dan Hill and Vonda Sheppard, from the album *Can't We Try* (Columbia, 87). Canadian balladeer Hill wrote this song with his wife.

Can'tcha Say (You Believe in Me)
Words and music by J. Green, Tom Scholz, and Brad Delp.
Hideaway Hits, 1987/Perceptive.
Best-selling record by Boston, from the album *Third Stage* (MCA, 87).

Caravan of Love
Revived in 1987 by the Housemartins, whose a cappella version went to number one in England, but is not included on their album (Go Discs, 86). See *Popular Music, 1920-1979.*

Carrie (Swedish)
English words and music by Joey Tempest and M. Michael.
Screen Gems-EMI Music Inc., 1986.
Best-selling record by Europe, from the album *The Final Countdown* (Epic, 86).

Carry the Torch
Words and music by Paul Davis and Doug Erikson.
Flip 'n' Dog, 1987.
Introduced by FireTown, from the album *In the Heart of the Heart Country,* (Atlantic, 87). When originally released on an independent extended-play record, the song was hailed by critics, resulting in a deal with a major label.

Casanova
Words and music by Reggie Calloway.
Calloco, 1987/Hip-Trip Music Co.
Best-selling record by Levert, from the album *The Big Throwdown* (Atlantic, 87). Nominated for a Grammy Award, Rhythm 'n' Blues Song of the Year, 1987.

Catch Me (I'm Falling)
Words and music by Jade Starling and Whey Cooler.
Genetic, 1987.
Best-selling record by Pretty Poison, from the album *Hiding Out* (Virgin, 87); also on the soundtrack of the film *Hiding Out.*

Causing a Commotion
Words and music by Madonna and Steve Bray.

WB Music Corp., 1987/Webo Girl Music/WB Music Corp./Bleu Disque Music/Black Lion.
Best-selling record by Madonna, from the album (Sire, 87) and film *Who's That Girl?*, in which she starred.

Celestial Soda Pop
Music by Ray Lynch.
Introduced by Ray Lynch on the album *Deep Breakfast* (MusicWest, 86), this popular instrumental received heavy play on "new age" radio, programming much in vogue with yuppies.

Change with the Changing Times
Words and music by Peter Holsapple.
Holsapple, 1987/I.R.S.
Introduced by Dbs, from the album *The Sound of Music* (IRS, 87).

Cherry Bomb
Words and music by John Cougar Mellencamp.
Riva Music Ltd., 1987.
Best-selling record by John Cougar Mellencamp, from the album *The Lonesome Jubilee* (Polygram, 87).

Christmas (Baby Please Come Home)
Words and music by Phil Spector, Ellie Greenwich, and Jeff Barry.
Mother Bertha Music, Inc./Trio Music Co., Inc.
Revived in 1987 by U2 for the album *A Very Special Christmas* (A & M), proceeds from which were donated to the Special Olympics. The song was originally record by Darlene Love, who sings back-up on the more recent version.

Christmas in Hollis
Words and music by Joseph Simmons, D. McDaniels, and Jason Mizell.
Protoons Inc., 1987/Rush Groove.
Introduced by Run DMC on the album *A Very Special Christmas* (A & M), this song offers a rap treatment of holiday sentiments.

City of Crime
Words and music by Peter Aykroyd, Dan Aykroyd, and Pat Thrall.
Swirling Vortex, 1987/Applied Action/Enthralled.
Introduced by Dan Aykroyd and Tom Hanks in the film and on the soundtrack album *Dragnet* (China/Chrysales, 87). A rap song.

Close to the Wind (English)
Words and music by Stuart Marson.
Misty River Music Ltd., England, 1987.
Performed by Fairport Convention on the album *In Real Time (Live '87)* (Island, 87).

Cloudbusting (English)
Words and music by Kate Bush.
Screen Gems-EMI Music Inc., 1986.
Introduced by Kate Bush on the album *The Whole Story* (EMI-America, 86), another unsuccessful attempt to capture a large U.S. audience for this quirky English composer.

Cold Hearts/Closed Minds
Words and music by Nanci Griffith.
Wing & Wheel, 1987.
Introduced by Nanci Griffith on the album *Lone Star State of Mind* (MCA, 87), a pleasant combination of country and folk-rock influences.

Come As You Are
Words and music by Peter Wolf and Tim Mayer.
Pal-Park Music, 1987.
Best-selling record by Peter Wolf, former lead singer of the J. Geils Band, from the album *Come As You Are* (EMI, 87).

Come Go with Me
Words and music by Lewis Martinee.
Panchin, 1987.
Best-selling record by Expose, from the album *Exposure* (Arista, 87).

Could've Been
Words and music by Lois Blaisch.
George Tobin, 1987.
Best-selling record by Tiffany, from the album *Tiffany* (MCA, 87).

Crazy from the Heart
Words and music by David Bellamy and Don Schlitz.
Bellamy Brothers Music, 1987/Don Schlitz Music.
Best-selling record by the Bellamy Brothers, from the album *Crazy from the Heart* (MCA/Curb, 87).

Crazy Man Michael (English)
Words and music by Richard Thompson and Dave Swarbrick.
Sparta Music, London, England/Island Music, 1987.
Performed by Fairport Convention, from the album *In Real Time (Live '87)* (Island, 87). Co-author Thompson is a former member of this legendary English folk group.

Crazy World
Words and music by Michael Rupert and Jerry Colker.
Introduced by Mara Getz and Michael Rupert in the 1987 musical

Mail, produced in Los Angeles and scheduled for Broadway in 1988. The same authors previously scored off Broadway with *Three Men Naked from the Waist Down.*

Criminal (Theme from *Fatal Beauty*)
Words and music by Sylvester LeVay and Tom Whitlock.
GMPC, 1987/Levay.
Introduced by Shannon on the soundtrack of the film *Fatal Beauty;* also appears on its soundtrack album.

Cross My Broken Heart
Words and music by Stephen Bray and Tony Pierce.
Famous Music Corp., 1987/Black Lion.
Best-selling record the Jets from the film and soundtrack album *Beverly Hills Cop II* (MCA, 87).

Cry Freedom
Music by George Fenton and Jonas Gwangwa.
MCA, Inc., 1987.
Introduced by George Fenton and Jonas Gwangwa in the film and on the soundtrack album of *Cry Freedom* (MCA, 87). Nominated for an Academy Award, Best Original Song, 1987.

Cry Little Sister (Theme from *The Lost Boys*)
Words and music by Mike Mainieri and Gerard McMann.
Warner-Tamerlane Publishing Corp., 1987/Hot Corner/WB Music Corp.
Introduced by Gerard McMann, from the film and soundtrack album *The Lost Boys* (Atlantic, 87).

Cry Myself to Sleep
Words and music by Paul Kennerly.
Irving Music Inc., 1986.
Best-selling record by the Judds from the album *Rockin' with the Rhythm* (RCA/Curb, 86).

D

Day in--Day Out (English)
Words and music by David Bowie.
Jones Music Co., 1987.
Best-selling record by David Bowie, from the album *Never Let Me Down* (EMI, 87).

Dear God (English)
Words and music by Andy Partridge.
Virgin Nymph, 1987.
Best-selling record by XTC, from the album *Skylarking* (Geffen, 86); although it was not on the original U.S. version of the album, it was added to later pressings after generating controversy for the agnosticism of its lyrics and achieving high sales asa twelve-inch single in the U.S. (it had been released as a B-side in England).

Dear Mr. Jesus
Words and music by R. Klender.
Klenco, 1986.
Introduced by by PowerSource, from the album *Shelter from the Storm* (PowerSource, 86). Featuring the voice of nine-year-old Sharon Batts, this poignant song deals with one of the year's most compelling issues, child abuse.

Deeper Love
Words and music by Diane Warren.
Realsongs, 1987.
Introduced by Meli'sa Morgan on the soundtrack of the film *The Golden Child* and its album (Capitol, 87).

Detox Mansion
Words and music by Warren Zevon and Jorge Calderon.
Zevon Music Inc., 1987.
Introduced by Warren Zevon on the album *Sentimental Hygiene*

39

(Virgin, 87). The song details Zevon's struggle toward recovery from alcoholism.

Diamonds
Words and music by Jimmy Jam (pseudonym for James Harris) and Terry Lewis.
Flyte Tyme Tunes, 1987.
Best-selling record by Herb Alpert, featuring Janet Jackson as lead singer; from the album *Keep Your Eye on Me* (A & M, 87).

Diamonds on the Soles of Her Shoes (American-South African)
English words and music by Paul Simon and Joseph Shabalala.
Paul Simon Music, 1986.
Best-selling record by Paul Simon, from the album *Graceland* (Warner Bros., 86), which won a Grammy Award as best album of the year. In the album Simon adapted many elements of South African street music and here collaborated with a noted musician from that country.

Didn't We Almost Have It All
Words by Will Jennings, music by Michael Masser.
Prince Street Music, 1987/Willin' David/Blue Sky Rider Songs.
Best-selling record by Whitney Houston, from the album *Whitney* (Arista, 87). Nominated for a Grammy Award, Song of the Year, 1987.

(I Just) Died in Your Arms (English)
Words and music by Nick Eede.
Virgin Nymph, 1987.
Best-selling record by Cutting Crew, from the album *Broadcast* (Virgin, 87).

Dinner with Gershwin
Words and music by Brenda Russell.
WB Music Corp., 1987/Geffen Music/Rutland Road.
Best-selling record Donna Summer, from the album *All Systems Go* (Geffen, 87). This was one of a number of releases marking the fiftieth anniversary of the death of songwriter George Gershwin, among them, new recordings of his musicals *Let Them Eat Cake* and *Of Thee I Sing* and opera star Kiri Te Kanawa's album *Kiri Sings Gershwin* (Angel/EMI), which made use of original orchestrations newly discovered in a Secaucus, New Jersey, warehouse.

Do Ya'
Words and music by K. T. Oslin.
Wooden Wonder, 1987.

Best-selling record by K. T. Oslin, from the album *80's Ladies* (RCA, 87).

Do You Hear What I Hear
Words and music by Noel Regney and Gloria Shayne.
Regent Music, 1962, 1979.
Revived in 1987 by Whitney Houston on the album *A Very Special Christmas* (A & M), this song was originally a best-seller for Bing Crosby. Co-author Regney also wrote the English lyrics for the 1963 hit by the Singing Nun, "Dominique" (see *Popular Music, 1920-1979*).

Doing It All for My Baby
Words and music by Phil Cody (pseudonym for Phil Feliciato) and M. Duke.
Bibo Music Publishers, 1986/Zookini/Vogue Music/Bob-a-Lew Songs.
Best-selling record by Huey Lewis and the News, from the album *Fore* (Chrysalis, 86); this was the fifth top-ten single for the album.

Dominoes
Words and music by Robbie Nevil, Barry Eastman, and Bobby Hart.
MCA Music, 1986/Bobby Hart.
Best-selling record by Robbie Nevil, from the album *Robbie Nevil* (Manhattan, 86).

Don't Come Inside My Head
Words and music by Elizabeth Swados.
Blackwood Music Inc., 1987.
Introduced by by Maribel Lizardo in the 1987 musical *Swing.*

Don't Disturb This Groove
Words and music by Mic Murphy and David Frank.
Science Lab, 1987.
Best-selling record by System, from the album *Don't Disturb This Groove* (Capitol, 87).

Don't Dream It's Over (Australian)
Words and music by Neil Finn.
Roundhead, 1987.
Best-selling record by Crowded House, from their album *Crowded House* (Capitol, 87). This song made a breakthrough single for singer-author Finn, who earlier had some fine efforts with Split Enz.

Don't Give Up (English)
Words and music by Peter Gabriel.
Cliofine, England, 1986/Hidden Pun.
Introduced by Peter Gabriel and Kate Bush on the album *So* (Geffen, 86).

Don't Go
Words and music by Marlon Jackson.
Vabritmar, 1987.
Best-selling record by Marlon Jackson, from the album *Baby Tonight* (Capitol, 87).

Don't Go to Strangers
Words and music by J. D. Martin and Russell Smith.
MCA Music, 1986.
Best-selling record by T. Graham Brown; from the album *I Tell It Like It Used to Be* (Capitol, 86).

Don't Make Me Wait for Love
Words and music by Preston Glass, Narada Michael Walden, and W. Afanasieff.
Bellboy Music, 1986/Gratitude Sky Music, Inc.
Best-selling record by Kenny G., with vocal by Kenny Williams, from the album *Duotones* (Arista, 87).

Don't Mean Nothin
Words and music by Richard Marx and Bruce Gaitsch.
ChiBoy, 1987/Edge of Fluke.
Best-selling record by Richard Marx, from the album *Richard Marx* (Manhattan, 87). Co-author and performer Marx is an accomplished studio musician and jingle writer.

Don't You Want Me
Words and music by Franne Golde, D. Bryant, and Jody Watley.
Bellboy Music, 1987/Gratitude Sky Music, Inc.
Best-selling record by Jody Watley, from the album *Jody Watley* (MCA, 87); this was the first solo effort from Watley, a former member of Shalamar.

Downtown Train
Words and music by Tom Waits.
Jalma, 1985.
Introduced by Tom Waits in the movie *Down by Law* ('86). Revived in 1987 by Patty Smythe in the album *Never Enough* (Columbia) and Mary Chapin Carpenter in the album *Hometown Girl* (Columbia, 87).

Dragnet
Music by Earl Schuman.
CBS-Robbins, 1953, 1981/Intersong, USA Inc.
Introduced by Art of Noise in the film and on the soundtrack album
  Dragnet (China/Chrysalis, 87).

Dream Warriors
Words and music by George Lynch and Jeff Pilson.
Megadude, 1987/E/A.
Introduced by Dokken in the movie *A Nightmare on Elm Street,
  Part 3,* (87). Featured on their album *Back for the Attack* (Elektra,
  87).

Dreamtime (English)
Words and music by The Stranglers.
CBS Songs Ltd., London, England, 1986/Plumbshaft Ltd., England.
Introduced by the Stranglers, on the album *Dreamtime* (Epic, 87).

Drink with Me to Days Gone By (French-English)
English words by Herbert Kretzmer, French words and music by
  Alain Boublil, music by Claude-Michel Schonberg.
Alain Boublil Music Inc., 1980, 1986.
Introduced by Anthony Crivello and company in the 1987 Broad-
  way production on *Les Miserables.*

Dude (Looks Like a Lady)
Words and music by Steven Tyler, Joe Perry, and Desmond Child.
Aerodynamics, 1987/Desmobile Music Co./April Music, Inc.
Best-selling record by Aerosmith, from the album *Permanent
  Vacation* (Geffen, 87). The song was nearly called "Cruisin' for
  the Ladies," but returned to this, its original title, in a rewrite.

Dungeons and Dragons
Words by Michael Champagne, music by Elliot Weiss.
Bittersuite Co., 1987.
Introduced by Joy Franz in the 1987 musical *Bittersuite.*

E

Earn Enough for Us (English)
Words and music by Andy Partridge.
Virgin Nymph, 1986.
Introduced by XTC on the album *Skylarking* (Geffen, 86), this song
offers the underrated writer's perennial complaint.

80's Ladies
Words and music by K. T. Oslin.
Wooden Wonder, 1987.
Best-selling record by K. T. Oslin, from the album *80's Ladies*
(RCA, 87). Nominated for a Grammy Award, Country Song of
the Year, 1987.

Elvis Is Everywhere
Words and music by MoJo Nixon.
Muffin Stuffin, 1987/La Rana.
Introduced by MoJo Nixon and Skid Roper on the album
Bo-Day-Shus (Enigma, 87), this song's satirical lyrics offer
inspired commentary on both Presleymania and the more recent
popular passion for television star Michael J. Fox.

Even a Dog Can Shake Hands
Words and music by Warren Zevon, Peter Buck, Mike Mills, and
Bill Berry.
Night Garden Music, 1987/Unichappell Music Inc.
Introduced by Warren Zevon on the album *Sentimental Hygiene*
(Island, 87). Zevon's co-authors are members of folk-rock group
REM.

Ever Since the World Ended
Words and music by Mose Allison.
Audre Mae Music, 1987.
Introduced by Mose Allison on the album *Ever Since the World*

Ended (Blue Note, 87), this song provides an optimistic report from one of music's most delightfully cynical observers.

Everchanging Times
Words and music by Burt Bacharach, Carole Bayer Sager, and Bill Conti.
United Artists Music Co., Inc., 1987/April Music, Inc./New Hidden Valley Music Co./Carole Bayer Sager Music/United Lion Music Inc./Blackwood Music Inc.
Introduced by Siedah Garrett on the album *Baby Boom;* there is also a single out on Quest Records (87).

Every Little Kiss
Words and music by Bruce Hornsby.
Zappo Music, 1986/Bob-a-Lew Songs.
Best-selling record by Bruce Hornsby and the Range, from the album *The Way It Is* (RCA, 86); this song became a hit on its second release, after Hornsby won a Grammy Award for Best New Artist of the Year.

Expressway to Your Heart
Revived in 1987 by the Breakfast Club, from their album *The Breakfast Club* (MCA). See *Popular Music, 1920-1979.*

F

Faith (English)
Words and music by George Michael.
Morrison Leahy, England/Chappell & Co., Inc., 1987.
Best-selling record by George Michael, from the album *Faith*
(Columbia, 87).

Fake
Words and music by Jimmy Jam (pseudonym for James Harris) and
Terry Lewis.
Flyte Tyme Tunes, 1987/Avant Garde Music Publishing, Inc.
Best-selling record by Alexander O'Neal, from the album *Hearsay*
(Tabu, 87). The songwriters are former members of the Time
(which was originally called Flyte Tyme).

Fallen Angel
Words and music by Robbie Robertson and Martin Page.
Medicine Hat Music, 1987/Martin Page/Zomba Enterprises, Inc.
Introduced by Robbie Robertson on his album *Robbie Robertson*
(Geffen, 87), this song is dedicated to Richard Manuel, Robert-
son's former colleague in the Band, who had committed suicide.

Falling for You for Years
Words and music by Troy Seals and Mike Reed.
WB Music Corp., 1987/Two-Sons Music/Lodge Hall Music, Inc.
Best-selling record by Conway Twitty, from the album *Borderline*
(MCA, 87).

Far Away Lands
Words and music by David Pomeranz, music by Peter Schless.
Marilor Music, 1987/Upward Spiral/Lincoln Pond Music.
Introduced by by David Pomeranz and Sasha Malinin (Cypress,
87), in an example of artistic detente between U.S. and Russian
musicians.

Fewer Threads than These
Words and music by Bucky Jones, Kevin Welch, and Gary Nichol-son.
Cross Keys Publishing Co., Inc., 1987.
Best-selling record by Holly Dunn, from the album *Cornerstone* (MTM, 87), this song was previously recorded by Dan Seals.

(You Gotta) Fight for Your Right (to Party)
Words and music by Beastie Boys, words and music by Rick Rubin.
Def Jam, 1986/Brooklyn Dust.
Best-selling record in 1987 by the Beastie Boys, from the album *Licensed to Ill* (Def Jam, 86). White rap's finest joke band pro-duced its only anthem with this song and lived it to the fullest in 1987.

The Final Countdown (Swedish)
English words and music by Joey Tempest.
Screen Gems-EMI Music Inc., 1986.
Best-selling record by Europe, from the album *The Final Countdown* (Epic, 86).

The Finer Things
Words by Will Jennings, music by Steve Winwood.
F.S. Ltd., England, 1986/WB Music Corp./Willin' David/Blue Sky Rider Songs.
Best-selling record by Steve Winwood, from the album *Back in the High Life* (Island, 86).

First We Take Manhattan (Canadian)
Words and music by Leonard Cohen.
Stranger Music Inc.
Performed by Jennifer Warnes on the album *Famous Blue Raincoat* (Cypress, 86). With this collection of Cohen's songs, Warnes became the foremost interpreter of the Canadian poet's world since Judy Collins.

Fishin in the Dark
Words and music by Wendy Waldman and Jim Photoglo.
Screen Gems-EMI Music Inc., 1986/Moon & Stars Music/Burger Bits.
Best-selling record by the Nitty Gritty Dirt Band, from the album *Hold On* (Warner Bros., 86). With this title, singer-songwriter Waldman broke away from the Los Angeles mold to make a successful transi-tion to Nashville collaborator.

Flames of Paradise
Words and music by Bruce Roberts and Andy Goldmark.
Broozertoones, Inc., 1987/Nonpariel Music.

Best-selling record by Jennifer Rush and Elton John, from the album *Heart Over Mind* (Epic, 87).

Flight of the Snowbirds, see Love Lights the World (Rendezvous)

For the Sake of the Song
Words and music by Townes Van Zandt.
Will Music, 1987.
Introduced by Townes Van Zandt on the album *At My Window* (Sugar Hill, 87), marking the legendary, grizzled country-folk writer's return to recording after a long absence.

Ford Econoline
Words and music by Nanci Griffith.
Wing & Wheel, 1987.
Introduced by Nanci Griffith on the album *Lone Star State of Mind* (MCA, 87).

Forever and Ever, Amen
Words and music by Paul Overstreet and Don Schlitz.
Writer's Group Music, 1987/Scarlet Moon Music/Don Schlitz Music.
Best-selling record by Randy Travis, from the album *Always and Forever* (Warner Bros., 87). Won a Country Music Association Award, Country Song of the Year, 1987; a Grammy Award, Country Song of the Year, 1987.

Fourth of July
Words and music by Dave Alvin.
Blue Horn Toad, 1987.
Recorded by X on the album *See How We Are* (Elektra, 87). Introduced by Dave Alvin, formerly the guitarist for X, on the album *Romeo's Escape* (Epic, 87).

From a Distance
Words and music by Julie Gold.
Julie Gold Music, 1987/Wing & Wheel.
Introduced by Nanci Griffith on the album *Lone Star State of Mind* (MCA, 87), this is one of the strongest country songs of the year.

Funkytown
Revived in 1987 by Pseudo Echo, from the album *Love an Adventure* (RCA). See *Popular Music, 1980-1984.*

G

The Gift (Canadian)
Words and music by Ian Tyson.
Slick Fork Music, 1987.
Introduced by Ian Tyson, formerly a member of the Canadian folk
   duo Ian and Sylvia, on the album *Cowboyography* (Sugar Hill,
   87). Tyson also wrote "Someday Soon" for Judy Collins.

Girls, Girls, Girls
Words and music by Tommy Lee, Nikki Sixx, and Mick Mars.
Motley Crue, 1987/Mick Mars/Krell/Sikki Nixx.
Best-selling record by Motley Crue, from the album *Girls, Girls,
   Girls* (Elektra, 87).

The Girls I Never Kissed
Words and music by Mike Leiber and Jerry Stoller.
Introduced by Frank Sinatra and Paul Anka (Reprise, 87). With this
   single, the label's founding artist, Sinatra, helped celebrate its
   return to the marketplace.

Go See the Doctor
Words and music by Moe Dewese.
Willesden Music, Inc., 1987.
Introduced by Kool Moe Dee on his album *Kool Moe Dee*
   (Rooftop/Jive, 87); in this song, written in the lobby of a New
   York City health clinic, the streetwise rapper reacts to the current
   climate of sexual caution.

God Will
Words and music by Lyle Lovett.
Michael H. Goldsen, Inc., 1986/Lyle Lovett.
Best-selling record by Lyle Lovett, one of country's finest new
   writer-performers, from his album *Lyle Lovett* (MCA, 86).

Good Times (Australian)
Words and music by Dave Faulkner.
Copyright Control, 1987.
Introduced by the Hoodoo Gurus on the album *Lose Your Cool* (Elektra, 87).

Good Times (Australian)
Words and music by George Young and Harry Vanda.
CBS Unart Catalog Inc., 1987.
Best-selling record by Inxs and Jimmy Barnes, from the movie *The Lost Boys* and its soundtrack album (Atlantic, 87). This songwriting team has been responsible for many hits, including "Friday on My Mind," by the Easybeats.

Goodbye Saving Grace
Words and music by Jon Butcher.
Grand Pasha, 1987.
Best-selling record by Jon Butcher, from the album *Wishes* (Capitol, 87).

Got My Mind Set on You
Words and music by Rudy Clark.
Carbert Music Inc.
Originally recorded in the 1960's, this best-selling revival by George Harrison was the first hit from his comeback album, *Cloud Nine* (Dark Horse, 87).

Gotta Serve Somebody
Words and music by Bob Dylan.
Special Rider Music, 1979.
Revived in 1987 by Luther Ingram (Profile), in 1986 this song earned Bob Dylan his only Grammy Award.

Graceland
Best-selling record by Paul Simon from his *Graceland* album. The album won the Grammy Award as Album of the Year in 1986; see *Popular Music 1986.* Won a Grammy Award, Best Record of the Year, 1987.

Green Hills of Earth
Words and music by David Frishberg.
Swiftwater Music, 1987.
A space-age lament performed by David Frishberg, the supper club balladeer, on the album *Can't Take You Nowhere* (Fantasy, 87).

Gypsy
Words and music by Suzanne Vega.
AGF Music Ltd., 1987/Waifersongs Ltd.

Introduced by Suzanne Vega on the album *Solitude Standing* (A & M), this last remaining vestage of the artist's folk music heritage on her 1987 album failed to make the charts when released as a single.

H

Had a Dream About You, Baby
Words and music by Bob Dylan.
Special Rider Music, 1987.
Introduced by Bob Dylan in the film *Hearts of Fire* and on the
album of the same title (Columbia, 87). Dylan portrayed a reclu-
sive former rock star in his first film appearance since *Pat Garrett
and Billy the Kid.*

Half Past Forever (Till I'm Blue in the Heart)
Words and music by Tom Brasfield.
Rick Hall Music, 1986.
Best-selling record by T. G. Sheppard from the album *It Still Rains
in Memphis* (Columbia, 86).

Hang on St. Christopher
Words and music by Tom Waits.
Ackee Music Inc.
Performed by Tom Waits on the album *Frank's Wild Years* (Island,
87), which comprised songs based on Waits's earlier play of the
same title.

Happy
Words and music by David Townshend, Bernard Jackson, and
David Conley.
Brampton Music Ltd., England, 1987.
Best-selling record by Surface, from the album *Surface* (Columbia,
87).

Happy Hour (English)
Words and music by P. D. Heaton and Stan Cullimore.
Go! Discs Ltd., England, 1986.
Introduced by by the Housemartins on the album *London 0 Hull 4*
(Elektra, 86).

Happy Together
Revived in 1987 by the Turtles, who had the original hit in 1967, for the film *Making Mr. Right*. See *Popular Music, 1920-1979*.

Hard Day on the Planet
Words and music by Loudon Wainwright.
Snowden Music, 1986.
Introduced by by Loudon Wainwright on the album *More Love Songs* (Rounder, 87).

The Hardest Time
Words and music by David Hidalgo and Louie Perez.
Davince Music, 1987/No Ko Music.
Introduced by Los Lobos on the album *By the Light of the Moon* (Slash/WB, 87).

Have a Little Faith in Me
Words and music by John Hiatt.
Lillybilly, 1987/Bug Music.
Introduced by John Hiatt on the album *Bring the Family* (A & M, 87), the seventh solo album from this respected songwriter.

Have You Ever Loved Somebody
Words and music by Barry Eastmond and Terry Skinner.
Zomba Enterprises, Inc., 1986/Willesden Music, Inc.
Best-selling record by Freddie Jackson, from the album *Just Like the First Time* (Capitol, 86).

Have Yourself a Merry Little Christmas
Revived in 1987 by the Pretenders for the album *A Very Special Christmas*. See *Popular Music, 1920-1979*.

Hazy Shade of Winter
Revived in 1987 by the Bangles on the soundtrack of the film *Less than Zero* and on its album. See *Popular Music, 1920-1979*.

Head to Toe
Words and music by Full Force.
Forceful Music, 1987/Willesden Music, Inc.
Best-selling record by Lisa Lisa and Cult Jam, from the album *Spanish Fly* (Columbia, 87).

Heart and Soul (English)
Words and music by Carol Decker and Ronnie Rogers.
Virgin Music, Inc., 1987.
Best-selling record by T'Pau; from the album *T'Pau* (Virgin, 87).
  Decker is the group's lead singer and Rogers, its former guitarist.

Heart Country
Words and music by Paul Davis and Doug Erikson.
Flip 'n' Dog, 1987.
Introduced by Firetown on the album *In the Heart of the Heart Country* (Atlantic, 87).

Heart Full of Soul
Revived in 1987 by Chris Isaak on the album *Chris Isaak* (Warner Bros.). See *Popular Music, 1920-1979.*

Heartbreak Beat (English)
Words and music by Richard Butler, Jon Aston, and Timothy Butler.
Blackwood Music Inc., 1987.
Best-selling record by the Psychedelic Furs, from the album *Midnight to Midnight* (Columbia, 87).

Hearts on Fire (Canadian)
Words and music by Bryan Adams and Jim Vallance.
Adams Communications, Inc., 1987/Calypso Toonz/Irving Music Inc.
Best-selling record by Bryan Adams, from the album *Into the Fire* (A & M, 87).

Heat of the Night (Canadian)
Words and music by Bryan Adams and Jim Vallance.
Adams Communications, Inc., 1987/Calypso Toonz/Irving Music Inc.
Best-selling record by Bryan Adams, from the album *Into the Fire* (A & M, 87). This song was inspired by a scene in the film *The Third Man.*

Heaven Is a Place on Earth
Words and music by Rick Nowels and Ellen Shipley.
Future Furniture, 1987/Shipwreck.
Best-selling record by Belinda Carlisle, from the album *Heaven on Earth* (MCA, 87).

Hello Stranger
Words by Doc Pomus, music by Mac Rebennack.
Skull Music, 1987/Stazybo Music.
Introduced by Marianne Faithfull on the album *Strange Weather* (Island, 87). Doc Pomus penned numerous hits in the 1950's for the Drifters and Dion and the Belmonts; Rebennack is the legendary Creole keyboard man, Dr. John.

Here I Go Again (English)
Words and music by David Coverdale and Bernie Marsden.

Seabreeze, 1983/CC/WB Music Corp.
Best-selling record by Whitesnake, from the album *Whitesnake* (Geffen, 87). In a different version, this song was a hit in Britain in 1982 on an album called *Saints and Sinners* that was not released in the United States.

Hey, Jack Kerouac
Words and music by Natalie Merchant and Robert Buck.
Christian Burial, 1987.
Introduced by 10,000 Maniacs on the album *In My Tribe* (Elektra, 87). This was the first song since Aztec Two-Step's "The Persecution and Resurrection of Dean Moriarity" to explore the Beatnik ethos espoused by Kerouac, author of the beat classic *On the Road.*

Hold Me
Words and music by Sheila Escovedo, Connie Guzman, and E. Minnifield.
Sister Fate Music, 1987/Pretty Man/Teete.
Best-selling record by Sheila E, from the album *Sheila E* (Paisley Park, 87).

The Homecoming Queen's Got a Gun
Words and music by Julie Brown, Terrence McNally, Charlie Coffey, and Ray Colcord.
Stymie Music, 1984.
Performed by Julie Brown on the album *Trapped in the Body of a White Girl* (Sire, 87). The song was previously featured on Brown's debut album, *Goddess in Progress.*

The Honey Thief (English)
Words and music by Bill McLeod, John McElhone, Graham Skinner, and Harry Travers.
Virgin Nymph, 1986.
Best-selling record in 1987 by Hipsway, from the album *Hipsway* (Columbia, 86).

Hourglass (English)
Words by Chris Difford, music by Glenn Tilbrook.
Virgin Music, Inc., 1987.
Best-selling record by Squeeze, from the album *Babylon and On* (A & M), this was the first hit song for the critically acclaimed songwriting duo.

House in Algiers (French)
English words by Julian More, music by Gilbert Becaud.
Introduced by Georgia Brown in the musical *Roza,* which had a short run on Broadway in 1987.

Housequake
Words and music by Prince Rogers Nelson.
Controversy Music, 1987.
Introduced by Prince in the film *Sign 'o' the Times* and on the album of the same title (Paisley Park, 87), with which the artist regained his popularity.

How Do I Turn You On
Words and music by Tom Reid and Robert Byrne.
Lodge Hall Music, Inc., 1986/Rick Hall Music.
Best-selling record in 1987 by Ronnie Milsap, from the album *Lost in the Fifties Tonight* (RCA, 86).

Hymne
Music by Vangelis.
WB Music Corp., 1987.
Performed by Joe Kenyon on the album *Hymne* (Mercury, 87); the music was originally used for a wine commercial.

Hypnotize Me
Words and music by Wang Chung.
Chong, England, 1987/Warner-Tamerlane Publishing Corp.
Best-selling record by Wang Chung from the album *Mosaic* (Geffen, 87). The song was introduced in the movie *Inner Space*.

I

I Ain't Ever Satisfied
Words and music by Steve Earle.
Goldline Music Inc., 1981.
Introduced by Steve Earle on *Exit 0* (MCA, 87), an album on the
rocking edge of country music.

I Cant Get Close Enough
Words and music by Sonny LeMaire and J. P. Pennington.
Tree Publishing Co., Inc., 1987/Pacific Island Music.
Best-selling record by Exile, from the album *Shelter from the Night*
(Epic, 87).

I Can't Stop Loving You
Words and music by Michael Jackson.
Mijac Music, 1987/Warner-Tamerlane Publishing Corp.
This best-selling record by Michael Jackson was the first hit from
his long-awaited album *Bad* (Epic, 87). The album entered the
charts at number one, but stayed there only a week.

I Can't Win for Losin' You
Words and music by Robert Byrne and Rick Bowles.
Rick Hall Music, 1986.
Best-selling record by Earl Thomas Conley, from the album *Too
Many Times* (RCA, 86).

I Could Never Take the Place of Your Man
Words and music by Prince Rogers Nelson.
Controversy Music, 1987.
Best-selling record by Prince, from the album *Sign 'o' the Times*
(Paisley Park, 87). Featured in the quasi-documentary film of the
same name.

I Do You
Words and music by Linda Mallah and Rick Kelly.

Meow Baby, 1987/Rick Kelly.
Best-selling record by the Jets, from the album *Magic* (MCA, 87).

I Don't Mind at All (English)
Words and music by Lyle Workman and Brent Bourgeois.
April Music, Inc., 1987/Lena May/Ackee Music Inc./Bourgeoise
   Zee.
Best-selling record by Bourgeois Tagg, from the album *Yo Yo*
   (Island, 87).

I Don't Wanna Know (English)
Words and music by John Martyn.
Warlock Music, 1978/Island Music.
An optimistic tune from the catalogue of an English soul writer,
   revived in 1987 by Richie Havens, one of the most soulful voices
   of the 1960's, on his album *Simple Things* (RBI, 87).

I Don't Want to Lose Your Love
Words and music by Gene McFadden, Linda Vitali, John White-
   head, and Jimmy McKinney.
Su-Ma Publishing Co., Inc., 1987/Bush Burnin' Music.
Best-selling record in 1987 by Freddie Jackson, from the album *Just
   Like the First Time* (Capitol, 86).

I Dreamed a Dream (French-English)
English words by Herbert Kretzmer, French words by Alain Boublil
   and Jean Marc Natel, music by Claude-Michel Schonberg.
Alain Boublil Music Inc., 1980, 1986.
Performed by Randy Graff in the 1987 Broadway production of *Les
   Miserables* and on the original cast album (Geffen, 87). Neil Dia-
   mond also recorded it on his album *Hot August Night II*
   (Columbia, 87).

I Eat Out
Words and music by Loudon Wainwright.
Snowden Music, 1986.
Introduced by Loudon Wainwright on the album *More Love Songs*
   (Rounder, 87), this song further details the life and times of the
   itinerant songwriter.

I Feel Good All Over
Words and music by Gabe Hardeman and Annette Hardeman.
Gabeson, 1987/On the Move.
Best-selling record by Stephanie Mills, from the album *If I Were
   Your Woman* (MCA, 87).

I Found Someone
Words and music by Michael Bolton and Mark Mangold.

April Music, Inc., 1987/Is Hot Music, Ltd./But For.
Best-selling record by Cher, from the album *Cher* (Geffen, 87).

I Go Crazy (English)
Words and music by James Mitchell, Kevin Mills, Nick Marsh, and Rocco Barker.
Nancy Hughes, 1987/Famous Music Corp.
Performed by Flesh for Lulu on the soundtrack of the film *Some Kind of Wonderful* and on its album (MCA,87); also featured on the group's album *Long Live the New Flesh* (Capitol, 87).

I Heard a Rumour (English)
Words and music by Sarah Dallin, Siobhan Fahey, Keren Woodward, Matt Aitken, Pete Waterman, and Mike Stock.
In A Bunch Music, London, England/Warner-Tamerlane Publishing Corp., 1987/Terrace Music.
Introduced by Bananarama in the film *Disorderlies* and on its soundtrack album (Tin Pan Apple/Polygram, 87); the group also had a best-selling record with the song. The trio of Stock, Aitken, and Waterman emerged in 1987 as one of the year's top producing teams.

I Heard It through the Grapevine
Revived in 1987 in an award-winning commercial for California raisins, featuring dancing claymation raisins led by the voice of drummer Buddy Miles. The "group," the California Raisins, subsequently released an album under the same name. See *Popular Music, 1920-1979* for further details on the song.

I Knew You Were Waiting (for Me) (English)
Words and music by Simon Climie and Dennis Morgan.
Chrysalis Music Corp., 1987/Rare Blue Music, Inc./Little Shop of Morgansongs.
Best-selling record in 1987 by Aretha Franklin and George Michael, from the album *Aretha* (Arista, 86).

I Know Him So Well (English)
This song from the English play *Chess,* which did not reach Broadway by the close of 1987, was revived in that year by Whitney Houston in a duet with her mother, Cissy Houston, on her album *Whitney* (Arista). For more information on the song, see *Popular Music 1985.*

I Know What I Like
Words and music by Chris Hayes and Huey Lewis.
Hulex Music.

Best-selling record in 1987 by Huey Lewis and the News, from the album *Fore* (Chrysalis, 86).

I Know Where I'm Going
Words and music by Don Schlitz, Craig Bickhardt, and Brent Maher.
MCA Music, 1987/Don Schlitz Music/Colgems-EMI Music Inc./April Music, Inc./Welbeck Music/Blue Quill Music.
Best-selling record by the Judds from the album *Heart Land* (MCA, 87).

I Like 'Em Big and Stupid
Words and music by Julie Brown, Terrence McNally, Charlie Coffey, and Ray Colcord.
Stymie Music, 1984.
Performed by Julie Brown on the album *Trapped in the Body of a White Girl* (Sire, 87), this song was introduced on her earlier record *Goddess in Progress.*

I Like My Body
Words and music by Gary Taylor.
Morning Crew, 1987.
Introduced by Chico De Barge in the film *Police Academy 4* and on the soundtrack album (Sire, 87).

I Looked in the Mirror
Words and music by Mose Allison.
Audre Mae Music, 1987.
Introduced by Mose Allison, the dean of American blues writers, on the album *Ever Since the World Ended* (Blue Note, 87).

I Love My Mom
Words and music by Suzzy Roche.
Deshufflin' Inc., 1987.
Introduced by the Roches in the play *Mama Drama* at the Ensemble Studio Theater in New York City in 1987. In addition to this previously unrecorded song written for the author's baby daughter, the production used three other songs by the Roche sisters.

I Need a Good Woman Bad
Words and music by Earl Thomas Conley.
April Music, Inc., 1987.
Introduced by Earl Thomas Conley on the album *Too Many Times* (RCA, 87).

I Need Love
Words and music by J. Smith, B. Erving, Darrell Pierce, Dwayne

Simon, and S. Etts.
Def Jam, 1987.
Best-selling record by LL Cool J, from the album *Bigger and Deffer* (Def Jam, 87).

I Prefer the Moonlight
Words and music by G. Chapman and M. Wright.
Riverstone, 1987/Blackwood Music Inc./Land of Music Publishing.
Best-selling record by Kenny Rogers, from the album *I Prefer the Moonlight* (RCA, 87).

I Still Haven't Found What I'm Looking For (Irish)
Words and music by U2.
Chappell & Co., Inc., 1987/U2.
Best-selling record by U2, this was the first hit from one of the year's most significant albums, *The Joshua Tree* (Island, 87). Nominated for a Grammy Award, Song of the Year, 1987.

I Think We're Alone Now
Revived in 1987 by Tiffany, on the album *Tiffany* (MCA); this was the first of two songs by Ritchie Cordell to make the charts in 1987, twenty years after this tune was a hit for Tommy James and the Shondells. See *Popular Music, 1920-1979* for further details.

I Wanna Dance with Somebody (Who Loves Me)
Words and music by Gary Merrill and Shannon Rubicam.
Irving Music Inc., 1986/Boy Meets Girl.
Best-selling record by Whitney Houston, from the album *Whitney* (Arista, 87). The artist turned again to the authors of "How Will I Know," one of the hits from her debut album, for the first big single from her long-awaited follow-up album.

I Wanna Go Back
Words and music by Danny Chauncey, Morty Byron, and Ira Walker.
Danny Tunes, 1987/Warner-Tamerlane Publishing Corp./Buy Rum/Raski/WB Music Corp.
Best-selling record in 1987 by Eddie Money, from the album *Can't Hold Back* (Columbia, 86).

I Want to Be Your Man
Words and music by Larry Troutman.
Troutman's Music, 1987/Saja Music.
Best-selling record by Roger, from the album *Unlimited* (Reprise, 87).

I Want to Know You Before We Make Love
Words and music by Candy Parton and Becky Hobbs.

Irving Music Inc., 1987/Beckaroo.
Best-selling record by Conway Twitty, from the album *Borderline* (MCA, 87).

I Want You Bad
Words and music by Terry Adams.
Tomato du Plenti, 1987/High Varieties.
Introduced by the Long Ryders on their album *Two Fisted Tales* (Island, 87). The author plays keyboards in NRBQ, a highly regarded "bar band," who have also recorded this song on their album *At Yankee Stadium.*

I Want Your Sex (English)
Words and music by George Michael.
Morrison Leahy, England/Chappell & Co., Inc., 1987.
Best-selling record by George Michael, from the album *Faith;* introduced on the soundtrack of the film *Beverly Hills Cop II* and on its soundtrack album (MCA, 87). The explicit title of this song sparked much controversy; its video was re-edited to discredit claims that it promoted promiscuity.

I Will Be There
Words and music by Tom Snow and Jennifer Kimball.
Snow Music, 1987/Michael H. Goldsen, Inc./Sweet Angel Music.
Best-selling record by Dan Seals, from the album *On the Front Line* (EMI-America, 87).

I Wonder Who She's Seeing Now
Words and music by Jimmy George and Lou Pardini.
Geffen Music, 1987/Lucky Break/Pardini.
Best-selling record by the Temptations, from the album *Together Again* (Motown, 87).

I Won't Forget You
Words and music by Bobby Dall, C. C. Deville, Brett Michael, and Rikki Rocket.
Sweet Cyanide, 1987/Willesden Music, Inc.
Best-selling record by Poison, from the album *Look What the Cat Dragged In* (Enigma, 87).

I Won't Need You Anymore (Always and Forever)
Words and music by Troy Seals and Max D. Barnes.
Warner-Tamerlane Publishing Corp., 1987/Face the Music/Blue Lake Music.
Best-selling record by Randy Travis, from the album *Always and Forever* (Warner Bros., 87).

I'd Still Say Yes
Words and music by Kenny Edmonds, Gary Scelsa, and Fenderella.
Now & Future, 1987/PSO Ltd./Klymaxx/Hip-Trip Music Co./Hip
   Chic.
Best-selling record by Klymaxx, from the album *Klymaxx* (MCA,
   87).

If She Would Have Been Faithful
Words and music by Randy Goodrum and Steve Kipner.
April Music, Inc., 1987/Stephen A. Kipner Music/California Phase
   Music.
Best-selling record by Chicago, from the album *18* (Warner Bros.,
   87).

I'll Be Alright without You
Words and music by Steve Perry, Jonathan Cain, and Neal Schon.
Colgems-EMI Music Inc., 1986.
Best-selling record in 1987 by Journey, from the album *Raised on
   Radio* (Columbia, 86).

I'll Be Your Baby Tonight
Revived in 1987 by Judy Rodman on the album *A Place Called
   Love* (MTM, 87). See *Popular Music 1920-1979.*

I'll Come Back as Another Woman (Icelandic)
English words and music by Bob Carpenter and Kent Robbins.
Let There Be Music Inc., 1985/Irving Music Inc.
Best-selling record in 1987 by Tanya Tucker, from the album *Girls
   Like Me* (Capitol, 86).

I'll Still Be Loving You
Words and music by Mary Ann Kennedy, Pat Bunch, Pam Rose,
   and Todd Cerney.
Warner-Tamerlane   Publishing   Corp.,   1986/Heart   Wheel/
   Chriswald Music/Hopi Sound Music/Chappell & Co., Inc.
Best-selling record in 1987 by Restless Heart, from the album
   Wheels (RCA, 86). Nominated for a Grammy Award, Country
   Song of the Year, 1987.

I'm in Love
Words and music by Paul Laurence and Timmy Allen.
Bush Burnin' Music, 1987/Willesden Music, Inc.
Best-selling record by Lillo Thomas, from the album *Lillo* (Capitol,
   87).

I'm No Angel
Words and music by Tony Colton and P. Palmer.
April Music, Inc., 1987/ATV Music Corp./Unichappell Music Inc.

Best-selling record by the Gregg Allman Band, from the album *I'm No Angel* (Epic, 87).

I'm Not Ashamed to Cry
Words and music by Jack Elliott.
Underdog, 1987.
Introduced by Ramblin' Jack Elliott on a 1987 record on the Bear Creek label; the singer-songwriter, whose folksinging inspired Bob Dylan and Arlo Guthrie in the 1960's, had gone many years without issuing a record until this one.

I'm Supposed to Have Sex with You
Words and music by Tonio K. (pseudonym for Steve Krikorian).
Famous Music Corp., 1987/Bibo Music Publishers/Evie Music Inc.
Introduced by Tonio K. on the soundtrack of the film *Summer School* and on its album; this notable Christian songwriter demonstrates a particularly cynical worldview.

In-A-Gadda-Da-Vida
Revived in 1987 by Slayer for the film and soundtrack album *Less than Zero* (Def Jam, 87). One of the earliest examples of the heavy metal sound was brought back by a second-generation band. See *Popular Music, 1920-1979.*

In God's Country (Irish)
Words and music by U2.
Chappell & Co., Inc., 1987/U2.
Best-selling record U2, from the album *The Joshua Tree* (Island, 87).

In My Dreams
Words and music by Kevin Cronin and Tom Kelly.
Fate Music, 1987/Denise Barry Music.
Best-selling record by REO Speedwagon, from the album *Life as We Know It* (Epic, 87).

In the Middle of the Land (Australian)
Words and music by Dave Faulkner.
Copyright Control, 1987.
Introduced by the Hoodoo Gurus on the album *Blow Your Cool* (Elektra, 87).

In This Love (English)
Words and music by David Coverdale and John Sykes.
Whitesnake, 1987/WB Music Corp.
Best-selling record by Whitesnake, from the album *Whitesnake* (Geffen, 87).

In Too Deep (English)
Words and music by Anthony Banks, Phil Collins, and Mike Rutherford.
Anthony Banks, England, 1986/Phil Collins, England/Mike Rutherford, England/Hit & Run Music.
Best-selling record by Genesis, from the album *Invisible Touch* (Atlantic, 86); this was the fifth single from this album to reach the top five.

Incident on 57th Street
Words and music by Bruce Springsteen.
Bruce Springsteen Publishing, 1987.
Performed by Bruce Springsteen and the E Street Band. A live version, released as the B-side of "Fire" has a playing time of ten minutes and three seconds, making it the longest B-side in history. The original studio version is on *The Wild, the Innocent, and the E Street Shuffle.*

It Takes a Little Rain
Words and music by Roger Murrah and Steve Dean.
Tom Collins Music Corp., 1987.
Best-selling record by the Oak Ridge Boys, from the album *Where the Fast Lane Ends* (MCA, 87).

It's a Sin (English)
Words and music by Nick Tennant and Chris Lowe.
Virgin Music, Inc., 1987.
Best-selling record by the Pet Shop Boys, from the album *Actually* (EMI-America, 87).

It's Getting Harder to Love You
Words and music by Michael Rupert and Jerry Colker.
Introduced by Mara Getz in the 1987 Los Angeles production of the musical *Mail.*

It's Gonna Be a Beautiful Night
Words and music by Prince Rogers Nelson.
Dramatis Music Corp., 1987.
Introduced by by Prince in the film and album *Sign 'o' the Times* (Paisley Park, 87).

It's Not Over ('Til It's Over)
Words and music by Robbie Nevil, John Van Torgeron, and Phil Galdston.
MCA Music, 1987/Tongerland/Kazoom.
Best-selling record by Starship, from the album *No Protection* (Grunt, 87).

It's the End of the World as We Know It (and I Feel Fine)
Words and music by Bill Berry, Peter Buck, Mike Mills, and Michael Stipe.
Night Garden Music, 1987/Unichappell Music Inc.
Introduced by R.E.M. on the album *Document* (IRS, 87), a national breakthrough for this favorite band of college audiences.

I've Been in Love Before (English)
Words and music by Nick Eede.
Virgin Nymph, 1987.
Best-selling record by Cutting Crew, from the album *Broadcast* (Virgin, 87).

I've Noticed a Change
Words and music by Douglas J. Cohen.
Introduced by June Gable, Liz Callahan, and Stephen Bogardus in *No Way to Treat a Lady* . The author received a Richard Rodgers development grant prior to the show's Broadway production.

J-K

Jam Tonight
Words and music by Freddie Jackson and Paul Laurence.
Wavemaker Music Inc., 1987.
Best-selling record in 1987 by Freddie Jackson, perhaps the most
    popular black ballad singer of the era, from the album *Just Like
    the First Time* (Capitol, 86). Jackson started out in a band called
    LJE with co-author Paul Laurence.

Jammin' Me
Words and music by Tom Petty, Mike Campbell, and Bob Dylan.
Gone Gator Music, 1987/Wild Gator Music/Special Rider Music.
Best-selling record by Tom Petty, from the album *Let Me Up I've
    Had Enough* (MCA, 87). This song was the product of a sponta-
    neous writing session by Dylan and Petty; Campbell, whose
    credits include "The Boys of Summer," was called in later to pol-
    ish the effort.

Jerusalem (English)
Words by William Blake, C. Hubert, and H. Parry, music by C.
    Hubert and H. Parry.
Robertson Publishing/Theodore Presser Co./Pub Pending 78.
Performed by Judy Collins on her album *Trust Your Heart* (Gold
    Castle, 87); the song, based on a poem by Blake, was originally
    from the 1981 film *Chariots of Fire.*

Jimmy Lee
Words and music by Jeffrey Cohen, Preston Glass, and Narada
    Michael Walden.
Gratitude Sky Music, Inc./Bellboy Music.
Best-selling record in 1987 by Aretha Franklin, from the album
    Aretha (Arista, 86).

Joe Stalin's Cadillac
Words and music by David Lowery.

Camper Von Beethoven Music, 1986.
Introduced by Camper Von Beethoven on the album *Camper Von Beethoven* (Pitch-A-Tent, 86). Author Lowery is the vocalist for this group, who were the underground favorites of the year.

Julia
Words and music by John Jarvis and Don Cook.
Tree Publishing Co., Inc., 1987/Cross Keys Publishing Co., Inc.
Best-selling record Conway Twitty, from the album *Borderline* (MCA, 87).

Jump Start
Words and music by Reggie Calloway and Vincent Calloway.
Colloco, 1987.
Best-selling record by Natalie Cole, from the album *Everlasting* (Manhattan, 87).

Just Like Fire Would (English)
Words and music by Chris Bailey.
Introduced by the Saints on the album *All Fool's Day* (TVT, 87).

Just the Facts
Words and music by Jimmy Jam (pseudonym for James Harris) and Terry Lewis.
MCA Music, 1987/Flyte Tyme Tunes.
Introduced by Patti La Belle on the soundtrack of the film *Dragnet* and on its album (MCA, 87).

Just to See Her
Words and music by Jimmy George and Lou Pardini.
Unicity Music, Inc., 1987/Lucky Break/Lars.
Best-selling record by Smokey Robinson, from the album *One Heartbeat* (Motown, 87). Nominated for a Grammy Award, Rhythm 'n' Blues Song of the Year, 1987.

Keep Your Hands to Yourself (English)
Best-selling record in 1987 by Georgia Satellites. See *Popular Music, 1986.*

The Kid Herself
Words by Fred Ebb, music by John Kander.
Fiddleback Music Publishing Co., Inc., 1987/Kander & Ebb Inc.
Introduced in the 1987 revival of *Flora, The Red Menace.* The song was written for the original production, but never used. Other numbers written for the new production are "Mister Just Give Me a Job," "The Joke," "I'm Keeping It Hot," and "Where Did Everybody Go."

Kids of the Baby Boom
Words and music by David Bellamy.
Bellamy Brothers Music, 1987.
Best-selling record by the Bellamy Brothers, from the album *Country Rap* (MCA/Curb, 87).

Kiss Him Goodbye, also known as **Na Na Hey Hey (Kiss Him Goodbye)**
Revived in 1987 by the Nylons, from the album *Happy Together* (Open Air/Windham Hill). The song was originally recorded by Steam; see *Popular Music, 1920-1979.*

L

La Bamba
Revived in 1987 by Los Lobos as the title song for the biographical film
about 1950's star Ritchie Valens; the Mexican-American band per-
forms the song in the film and on the soundtrack album (Slash/Warner
Bros., 87). "La Bamba" was originally the flipside of Valens's big hit
"Oh Donna"; its use in the film sparked renewed interest in Los Lobos
whose rendition of the song went to the top of the charts. See *Popular
Music, 1920-1979*.
Nominated for Grammy Awards, Best Record of the Year, 1987,
and Best Song of the Year, 1987.

La Isla Bonita
Words and music by Madonna, Patrick Leonard, and Bruce
Gaitsch.
WB Music Corp., 1986/Bleu Disque Music/Webo Girl
Music/WB Music Corp./Johnny Yuma/Edge of Fluke.
Best-selling record in 1987 by Madonna, from the album *True Blue*
(Warner Brothers, 86).

The Lady in Red (English)
Words and music by Chris DeBurgh.
Almo Music Corp., 1986.
Best-selling record in 1987 by Chris DeBurgh, from the album *Into
the Night* (A & M, 86). The song went to number one in England,
then became a hit in the United States upon its re-release here.

The Last One to Know
Words and music by Matraca Berg and Jane Mariash.
Tapadero Music, 1987/Cavesson Music Enterprises Co.
Best-selling record by Reba McEntire, from the album *The Last
One to Know* (MCA, 87).

Lean on Me
Revived in 1987 by Club Nouveau on the album *Life, Love, and*

Pain (Tommy Boy/Warner Bros., 86); this is a disco rendition of the Bill Withers hit. See *Popular Music, 1920-1979.* Nominated for a Grammy Award, Rhythm 'n' Blues Song of the Year, 1987.

Learning How to Love You
Words and music by John Hiatt.
Lillybilly, 1987.
Introduced by John Hiatt on the album *Bring the Family* (A & M, 87), of which it forms the centerpiece, according to Hiatt.

Learning to Fly (English)
Words and music by David Gilmour, Moore, Bob Ezrin, and Carin.
Pink Floyd, London, England.
Best-selling record by Pink Floyd, from the album *A Momentary Lapse of Reason* (Columbia, 87). The album marked a comeback for this major group of the 1970's.

Leave It All to Me
Words and music by Paul Anka, Alan Bergman, and Marilyn Bergman.
Paulanne Music Inc./Threesome Music.
Introduced by Frank Sinatra and Paul Anka (Reprise, 87). Anka teamed with the Oscar-winning husband-and-wife lyricists to create this song for Sinatra's return to the label he founded.

Leave Me Lonely
Words and music by Gary Morris.
Gary Morris Music, 1986.
Best-selling record in 1987 by Gary Morris, from the album *Plain Brown Wrapper* (Warner Bros., 86).

Lessons in Love (English)
Words and music by Mark King, Wally Badarou, and Phil Gould.
Level 42 Songs, 1987/Chappell & Co., Inc./Island Visual Arts.
Best-selling record by level 42, from the album *Running in the Family* (Polygram, 87).

Let Freedom Ring
Words and music by Bruce Sussman, Jack Feldman, and Barry Manilow.
Townsway Music, 1987/Appogiatura Music Inc./Camp Songs Music.
Introduced by Barry Manilow as the finale of the CBS television special *We the People 200,* celebrating the two hundredth anniversary of the Constitution.

Let It Be (English)
Revived in 1987 by Ferry Aid, an ad hoc group including Paul

McCartney, Mark Knopfler, Kate Bush, and Boy George, among others. Proceeds from the Profile-label record went to benefit the survivors of a ferry boat disaster in Zeebrugge, Belgium. See *Popular Music, 1920-1979.*

Let Me Be the One
Words and music by Lewis Martinee.
Panchin, 1987.
Best-selling record by Expose, from the album *Exposure* (Arista, 87).

Let Me Up I've Had Enough
Words and music by Tom Petty and Mike Campbell.
Gone Gator Music, 1987/Wild Gator Music.
Introduced by Tom Petty and the Heartbreakers on the album *Let Me Up I've Had Enough* (MCA, 87).

Let Us Begin, see What Are We Making Weapons For.

Lethal Weapon
Words and music by Michael Kamen.
Warner-Tamerlane Publishing Corp., 1987.
Introduced by Honeymoon Suite on the soundtrack of the movie *Lethal Weapon* and on its album (Warner Bros., 87).

Let's Go (English)
Words and music by Wang Chung.
Chong, England, 1987/Warner-Tamerlane Publishing Corp.
Best-selling record by Wang Chung, from the album *Mosaic* (Warner Bros., 87).

Let's Go to Heaven in My Car
Words and music by Brian Wilson, Eugene Landy, and Gary Usher.
Beach Bum, 1987/Fire Mist/Beachead.
Performed by Beach Boy Brian Wilson in a rare solo effort for the soundtrack of the film *Police Academy 4* and its album (Sire, 87). Wilson shares credit for the song with his therapist.

Let's Talk Dirty in Hawaiian
Words and music by John Prine and Fred Koller.
Spoondevil, 1987/Grandma Annie Music/Lucrative.
Introduced by John Prine, one of the premier singer-songwriters of the 1970's, on a record on the Oh Boy label. This novelty song ridicules censorship problems in the music business.

Let's Wait Awhile
Words and music by James Harris, Terry Lewis, Janet Jackson, and Reginald Andrews.

Flyte Tyme Tunes, 1986/Crush Club.
Best-selling record in 1987 by Janet Jackson, from her album
   Control (A & M, 86). When this single reached number one, Jackson became the first female artist to achieve five number one
   singles in a row.

Let's Work (English)
Words and music by Mick Jagger and Dave Stewart.
Promopub B. V., CH-1017 Amsterdam, Netherlands, 1987/BMG/
   Arista Music, Inc.
Introduced by Mick Jagger in the album *Primitive Cool* (Columbia,
   87), this song proved to be a big hit among devotees of aerobics.

The Letter, see Vanna, Pick Me a Letter.

Light at the End of the Tunnel (English)
Music by Andrew Lloyd Webber, words by Richard Stilgoe.
The Really Useful Group, England, 1987.
Introduced by the company of the musical *Starlight Express,* which
   opened on Broadway in 1987. Performed by Ritchie Havens on
   the album *Music and Songs from Starlight Express* (MCA, 87).

Light of Day
Words and music by Bruce Springsteen.
Bruce Springsteen Publishing.
Introduced in the film *Light of Day* by the Barbusters, the group
   created for the movie's storyline and fronted by its stars, Joan Jett
   and Michael J. Fox. Despite their presence and songs by Bruce
   Springsteen, neither the film nor its sound track album (MCA,
   87) was a hit.

Little Darlin'
Revived in 1987 by Dustin Hoffman and Warren Beatty as Chuck
   and Lyle in the film *Ishtar.* The release of this number as a single
   (on Capitol) marked the stars' recording debut, although Hoff-
   man had previously played a songwriter in the film *Who Is Harry
   Kellerman ... and Why Is He Saying Those Terrible Things about
   Me?* in which he sang tunes by Shel Silverstein. See *Popular
   Music, 1920-1979.*

The Little Drummer Boy
Revived in 1987 by Bob Seger, for the album *A Very Special
   Christmas* (A & M), which became the most successful holiday
   album ever. See *Popular Music, 1920-1979.*

Little Lies (English)
Words and music by Christine McVie and Eddy Quintela.
Fleetwood Mac Music Ltd., 1987.

Best-selling record by Fleetwood Mac, from the album *Tango in the Night* (Warner Bros., 87).

Live My Life
Words and music by Allee Willis and Danny Sembello.
Streamline Moderne, 1987/Texas City/No Pain, No Gain/Unicity Music, Inc.
Introduced by by Boy George in the film and soundtrack album *Hiding Out* (Virgin, 87).

Livin' on a Prayer
Words and music by Jon Bon Jovi, Richie Sambora, and Desmond Child.
Bon Jovi Publishing, 1986/Polygram Music Publishing Inc./April Music, Inc./Desmobile Music Co.
Despite nearly being left off the album *Slippery When Wet* (Polygram, 86), this song went on to be a best-seller for Bon Jovi, 1987.

The Living Daylights (English)
Words by Pal Waaktaar, music by John Barry.
ATV Music Corp., 1987/United Lion Music Inc.
Introduced by a-ha in the film and on the soundtrack album *The Living Daylights* (Warner Bros., 87). Waaktaar is a member of a-ha.

Living in a Box (English)
Words and music by M. Vere and S. Piggot.
Brampton Music Ltd., England/WB Music Corp., 1987.
Best-selling record by Living in a Box, from the album by the same title (Chrysalis, 87).

Living in the Promiseland
Words and music by David Lynn Jones.
Blue Water, 1985/Mighty Nice Music/Skunk Deville/David Lynn Jones.
Revived in 1987 by David Lynn Jones on the album *Hard Times on Easy Street* (Mercury). See *Popular Music 1986.*

Lone Star State of Mind
Words and music by Patrick Alger, Gene Levine, and Fred Koller.
Lucrative, 1987/Bait and Beer.
Introduced by Nanci Griffith on her album *Lone Star State of Mind* (MCA, 86).

Lonely Boy
Words and music by George Gershwin.
New World Music Corp. (NY).

Introduced by Cynthia Haymon and Ruby Hinds on the special television tribute to George Gershwin, *'S Wonderful*. The song was originally written for Ann Brown to sing in *Porgy and Bess*, but she rejected it in favor of "Summertime."

A Long Line of Love
Words and music by Paul Overstreet and Thom Schuyler.
Bethlehem.
Best-selling record by Michael Martin Murphey from the album *Americana* (Warner Bros., 87).

Long Slide (for an Out)
Words and music by Dan Zanes.
Of the Fire Music, 1987/Big Thrilling Music.
Introduced by the Del Fuegos on the album *Stand Up* (Slash/Warner Bros., 87).

The Longest Summer
Words and music by Wendy Waldman.
Moon & Stars Music, 1987/Screen Gems-EMI Music Inc.
Introduced by Wendy Waldman on the album *Letters Home* (Cypress, 87).

Looking at You (across the Breakfast Table)
Revived in 1987 by Michael Feinstein on the album *Michael Feinstein Sings Irving Berlin* (Columbia). See *Popular Music, 1920-1979.*

Looking for a New Love
Words and music by Andre Cymone and Jody Watley.
April Music, Inc., 1987/Intersong, USA Inc./Ultrawave.
Best-selling record by Jody Watley, from the album *Jody Watley* (MCA, 87), her first solo effort since leaving Shalamar. Watley received a Grammy as Best New Artist of the Year.

Lost in Emotion
Words and music by Full Force.
Forceful Music, 1987/Willesden Music, Inc./My My Music/Careers Music Inc.
Best-selling record by Lisa Lisa and Cult Jam, from the album *Spanish Fly* (Columbia, 87).

Love Is a House
Words and music by Martin Lascelles, Geoff Gurd, and G. Foster.
Tee Girl Music, 1987.
Introduced by the Force M.D.'s on the album *Touch and Go* (Tommy Boy, 87).

Love Is Being Loved
Words and music by Mickey Rooney.
Timic, 1987.
Introduced by Jan Rooney on the Silver Star label. The author and
singer are husband and wife.

Love Lights the World (Rendezvous), also known as **Flight of the
Snowbirds**
Words by Jeremy Lubbock and Linda Thompson Jenner, music by
David Foster.
Air Bear, 1987/Nero Publishing/Hollysongs.
Performed by David Foster and the Red Army chorus at Rendez-
vous '87 Peace Festival in Quebec City, Canada (Atlantic, 87).
This song originated on Foster's solo album as an instrumental
called "Flight of the Snowbirds," before the Red Army Choir
transformed it, with the help of the lyricists, into a song about
world peace.

Love Lives On
Words by Cynthia Weil and Will Jennings, music by Barry Mann
and Bruce Broughton.
MCA Music, 1987/Music Corp. of America.
Introduced by Joe Cocker on the soundtrack of the film *Harry and
the Hendersons* and on its album (MCA, 87).

(If You) Love Me Just a Little
Words and music by La La (pseudonym for Laforest Cope) and Full
Force.
Little Tanya, 1987/MCA Music/Forceful Music/Willesden Music,
Inc.
Best-selling record by La La, from the album *La La* (Arista, 86). La
La previously penned the Whitney Houston smash "You Give
Good Love."

Love Me Like You Used To
Words and music by Paul Davis and Bobby Emmons.
Web 4 Music Inc., 1987/Paul & Jonathan/Rightsong Music Inc./
Attadoo.
Best-selling record by Tanya Tucker, from the album *Love Me Like
You Used To* (Capitol, 87).

Love Power
Words by Carole Bayer Sager, music by Burt Bacharach.
New Hidden Valley Music Co., 1987/Carole Bayer Sager Music.
Best-selling record by Dionne Warwick, from the album
Reservations for Two (Arista, 87). This song marked a return by
Bacharach to writing for Warwick, as he had done with his prev-
ious partner, Hal David, throughout the 1960's. The 1986 Gram-

my-winning "That's What Friends Are For," which he helped write and Warwick joined in performing, had in fact been written for the 1982 film *Night Shift,* where it was performed by Rod Stewart.

Love Someone Like Me
Words and music by Holly Dunn and Radney Foster.
Lawyer's Daughter, 1987/Uncle Artie.
Best-selling record by Holly Dunn, from the album *Cornerstone* (MTM, 87).

Love, You Ain't Seen the Last of Me
Words and music by Kendall Franceschi.
WBM, 1987.
Best-selling record by John Schneider, from his *Greatest Hits* album (MCA, 87).

Love You Down
Words and music by Melvin Riley.
Music Corp. of America, 1986/Off Backstreet Music/Ready for the World Music/Trixie Lou Music.
Best-selling record in 1987 by Ready for the World, from the album *Long Time Coming* (MCA, 86).

Lovin' You
Words and music by Kenny Gamble and Leon Huff.
Downstairs Music, Inc., 1987/Piano/Mighty Three Music.
Best-selling record by the O'Jays, from the album *Let Me Touch You* (P.I.R., 87). This song marks the return of one of the major songwriting duos of the 1970's.

Luka
Words and music by Suzanne Vega.
Waifersongs Ltd., 1987/AGF Music Ltd.
Best-selling record by Suzanne Vega, from the album *Solitude Standing* (A & M, 87). This song about child abuse touched a nerve in a year when children in jeopardy generated major news stories throughout the country. Nominated for Grammy Awards, Best Record of the Year, 1987, and Best Song of the Year, 1987.

Lynda
Words and music by Bill LaBounty and Pat McLaughlin.
Screen Gems-EMI Music Inc., 1987.
Best-selling record by Steve Wariner, from his *Greatest Hits* album. (MCA, 87).

M

Make No Mistake, She's Mine, also known as **Make No Mistake,
  He's Mine,**
Words and music by Kim Carnes.
Moonwindow Music, 1985.
Revived in 1987 by Ronnie Milsap and Kenny Rogers on the album
  Heart and Soul (RCA, 87). Originally released as a single by the
  writer in a duet with Barbra Streisand, under the title "Make No
  Mistake, He's Mine."

Mama Don't Cry
Words by Michael Champagne, music by Elliot Weiss.
Bittersuite Co., 1987.
Introduced by Claudine Casson-Jellison in the musical *Bittersuite*
  ('87).

Mary's Prayer (Seychelles)
Words and music by Gary Clark.
Copyright Control, 1987.
Best-selling record by Danny Wilson (a group), from the album
  Meet Danny Wilson (Virgin, 87). Songwriter Clark is the vocalist
  of the group.

Maybe Your Baby's Got the Blues
Words and music by Troy Seals and Graham Lyle.
WB Music Corp., 1986/Two-Sons Music/Irving Music Inc.
Best-selling record in 1987 by the Judds, from the album *Heart
  Land* (RCA/Curb, 86).

Meet Me Half Way
Words by Tom Whitlock, music by Giorgio Moroder.
GMPC, 1987/Go Glow.
Best-selling record by Kenny Loggins. Introduced in the movie and
  on the soundtrack album *Over the Top* (Columbia, 87).

Meet on the Ledge (English)
Words and music by Richard Thompson.
Island Music.
Revived in 1987 by Fairport Convention on the album *In Real Time (Live '87)* This was a live remake of the group's traditional closing tune.

Midnight Blue
Words and music by Lou Gramm and Bruce Turgon.
Stray Notes Music, 1987/Colgems-EMI Music Inc./Acara.
Best-selling record by Lou Gramm, from the album *Ready or Not* (Atlantic, 87).

Mony Mony
Revived in 1987 by Billy Idol on the album *Vital Idol* (Chrysalis, 87). The second Ritchie Cordell-Tommy James song revived this year, this one was inspired by the Mutal of New York (MONY) building visible from James's apartment window. See *Popular Music, 1920-1979.*

The Moon Is Still Over Her Shoulder
Words and music by Hugh Prestwood.
Lawyer's Daughter, 1984.
Best-selling record in 1987 by Michael Johnson, from the album *Wings* (RCA, 86).

Moonlighting (Theme)
Best-selling record by Al Jarreau, from the album *Moonlighting* (RCA, 87). This television theme was first released as a single in England, where its success prompted the U.S. release. See *Popular Music 1986.* Nominated for a Grammy Award, Best Song for TV/ Movies, 1987.

Mornin' Ride
Words and music by Steve Bogard and Jeff Tweel.
Chappell & Co., Inc., 1987/Unichappell Music Inc.
Best-selling record in 1987 by Lee Greenwood, from the album *Love Will Find Its Way to You* (MCA, 86).

The Music of the Night (English)
Words by Charles Hart and Richard Stilgoe, music by Andrew Lloyd Webber.
The Really Useful Group, England, 1987/Colgems-EMI Music Inc.
Performed by Michael Crawford on the cast album of the musical *The Phantom of the Opera* (87). The show and song were hits in Britain before the Broadway opening in 1988.

My Baby Worships Me
Words and music by Steve Earle.
Goldline Music Inc., 1982, 1986.
Performed by Tom Principato on the album *Smokin'* (Powerhouse, 86).

My Forever Love
Words and music by Gerald Levert and Marc Gordon.
Ferncliff, 1987.
Best-selling record by Levert, from the album *The Big Throwdown* (Atlantic, 87).

My Little Buttercup
Words and music by Randy Newman.
OPC, 1986.
Introduced by Randy Newman in the film *Three Amigos* and its soundtrack album (Warner Bros., 86).

N

Na Na Hey Hey (Kiss Him Goodbye), see **Kiss Him Goodbye**

Navajo Rug (Canadian)
Words and music by Ian Tyson and Tom Russell.
Slick Fork Music, 1987/End of the Trail.
Best-selling record by Ian Tyson, from the album *Cowboyography*
  (Sugar Hill, 87).

Need You Tonight (Australian)
Words and music by Andrew Farriss and Michael Hutchence.
MCA Music, 1987.
Best-selling record by Inxs, from the album *Kick* (Atlantic, 87).

A New England (English)
Words and music by Billy Bragg.
Chappell & Co., Inc., 1983.
Introduced by Billy Bragg; collected on the album *Back to Basics*
  (Elektra, 87). This New Wave English folksinger exhibits a simple
  guitar-vocal style reminiscent of such 1960's protest singers as
  Phil Ochs. Kirsty MacColl had a hit in England with this song.

New Orleans Ladies
Revived in 1987 by Gabriel on the NSO label. See *Popular Music,
  1920-1979.*

News from Nowhere
Words and music by Dan Zanes.
Of the Fire Music, 1987/Big Thrilling Music.
Best-selling record by the Del Fuegos, from the album *Stand Up*
  (Slash/Warner Bros., 87).

Night After Night
Words and music by Bob Dylan.
Special Rider Music, 1987.
Introduced by Bob Dylan in the film *Hearts of Fire* and on its album
  (Columbia, 87).

No One Is Alone
Words and music by Stephen Sondheim.
Revelation Music Publishing Corp., 1987/Rilting Music Inc.
Introduced by Kim Crosby, Chip Zien, Ben Wright, and Danielle
    Ferland in the musical *Into the Woods,* which opened on Broad-
    way in 1987; original cast album is on RCA/Red Seal label.

No Place Like Home
Words and music by Paul Overstreet.
Writer's Group Music, 1986/Scarlet Moon Music.
Best-selling record in 1987 by Randy Travis, from the album
    Storms of Life (Warner Bros., 86).

No Reservations
Words and music by Bob Mould.
Husker Music, 1986.
Introduced by Husker Du on the album *Warehouse* (Warner Bros.,
    87).

No Way Out
Words and music by Paul Anka and Michael McDonald.
Paulanne Music Inc., 1987/Genevieve Music.
Introduced by Julia Migenes and Paul Anka as the title song for the
    1987 Columbia Pictures film *No Way Out.*

Nobody There But Me
Words and music by Bruce Hornsby.
Zappo Music, 1987/Bob-a-Lew Songs.
Introduced by Willie Nelson on the album *Island in the Sea*
    (Columbia, 87). Nelson's selection of this song confirmed Horns-
    by's emergence as an important songwriter.

Nobody's Fool
Words and music by Tom Keifer.
Chappell & Co., Inc., 1986/Eve.
Best-selling record in 1987 by Cinderella, from the album *Night
    Songs* (Mercury, 86).

Nothing's Gonna Change My Love for You
Words and music by Michael Masser.
Prince Street Music, 1985/Almo Music Corp./Screen Gems-EMI
    Music Inc.
Introduced by George Benson on his album *20/20* in 1985. Revived
    in 1987 by Glenn Medeiros on the album *Glenn Medeiros*
    (Amherst, 87).

Nothing's Gonna Stop Us Now
Words and music by Diana Warren and Albert Hammond.
Realsongs, 1987/Albert Hammond.
Best-selling record by Starship (Grant, 87); introduced in the 1987
film *Mannequin.* Nominated for an Academy Award, Best Original Song, 1987; a Grammy Award, Best Song for TV/Movies,
1987.

Nowhere Road
Words and music by Steve Earle and Reno Kling.
Goldline Music Inc., 1987.
Best-selling record by Steve Earle, from the album *Exit O* (MCA,
87).

O

Ocean Front Property
Words and music by Dean Dillon, Chuck Cochran, and Royce
 Porter.
Tree Publishing Co., Inc., 1987/Larry Butler Music Co./Southwing/
 Blackwood Music Inc.
Best-selling record by George Strait, from the album *Ocean Front
 Property* (MCA, 87).

Oh Yeah (West German)
Words and music by Boris Blank and Dieter Meier.
WB Music Corp., 1985.
Performed by Yello in the films *The Secret of My Success* ('87) and
 Ferris Bueller's Day Off ('86). Originally appeared on a 1985
 album.

Ohio Afternoon
Words and music by Mark Hardwick, Mike Craver, and Debbie
 Monk.
Introduced by Mark Hardwick, Mike Craver, Debbie Monk, and
 Mary Murfitt in the 1987 Off-Broadway production *Oil City
 Symphony.*

On My Own (French-English)
French words by Alain Boublil and Jean Marc Natel, English words
 by Herbert Kretzmer, music by Alain Boublil and Claude-Michel
 Schonberg.
Editions Musicales, Paris, France, 1980, 1986/Alain Boublil Music
 Inc.
Introduced by Frances Ruffelle in the London Production of *Les
 Miserables* and recreated on Broadway in 1987 where the perfor-
 mer won a Tony Award. Recorded on the Broadway cast album.
 Also sung by Elaine Paige on the album *Stages* (Atlantic, 87).

One for the Money
Words and music by B. Moore and M. Williams.
Tapadero Music, 1987/Cavesson Music Enterprises Co.
Best-selling record by T. G. Sheppard, from the album *One for the Money* (Columbia, 87).

One Heartbeat
Words by S. Legassick, music by B. Ray.
Chubu, 1987.
Best-selling record by Smokey Robinson, from the album *One Hearbeat* (Motown, 87).

The One I Love
Words and music by Bill Berry, Peter Buck, Mike Mills, and Michael Stipe.
Night Garden Music, 1987/Unichappell Music Inc.
Best-selling record by R.E.M. from the album *Document* (I.R.S., 87); this was the breakthrough single for the former underground band.

One Night Only
Revived in 1987 by Elaine Paige on the album *Stages* (Atlantic). For details on this song from the musical *Dreamgirls,* see *Popular Music, 1980-1984.*

One Promise Too Late
Words and music by Dave Loggins, Lisa Silver, and Don Schlitz.
MCA Music, 1987/Patchwork Music/Don Schlitz Music/Music Corp. of America.
Best-selling record by Reba McEntire, from her *Greatest Hits* album (MCA, 87).

One Step Up
Words and music by Bruce Springsteen.
Bruce Springsteen Publishing, 1987.
Introduced by Bruce Springsteen on the album *Tunnel of Love* (Columbia, 87). With this song about cheating, the singer-writer ventured in country music territory.

One Time One Night
Words and music by David Hidalgo and Louie Perez.
Davince Music, 1987/No Ko Music.
Introduced by Los Lobos on the album *By the Light of the Moon* (Slash/Warner Bros., 87).

Only in My Dreams
Words and music by Debbie Gibson.
Creative Bloc, 1987.

Best-selling record by Debbie Gibson, from the album *Out of the Blue* (Atlantic, 87). This was the sixteen-year-old pop music prodigy's first hit.

Only You (English)
Words by Richard Stilgoe, music by Andrew Lloyd Webber.
The Really Useful Group, England, 1987.
Introduced by Greg Mowry and Riva Rice in the 1987 Broadway production of *Starlight Express,* a show that made its debut in London. The song was also recorded by Peter Hewlett and Josie Aiello on the album *Music and Songs from "Starlight Express"* (MCA, 87).

Our Favorite Restaurant
Words by Michael Champagne, music by Elliot Weiss.
Bittersuite Co., 1987.
Introduced by Joseph Neil, John Jellison, Claudine Casson-Jellison, and Joy Franz in the musical *Bittersuite* (87).

Out of Love
Words and music by John Prine and Bill Caswell.
Big Ears Music Inc., 1987/Bruised Oranges/Black Sheep Music Inc.
Introduced by John Prine on the album *German Afternoons* (Oh Boy, 87); this song is a take-off on a popular beer commercial.

Out That Door (Australian)
Words and music by Dave Faulkner.
Copyright Control, 1987.
Introduced by the Hoodoo Gurus on the album *Blow Your Cool* (Electra, 87).

P

Paper in Fire
Words and music by John Mellencamp.
Riva Music Ltd., 1987.
Best-selling record by John Cougar Mellencamp, from the album
The Lonesome Jubilee (Mercury, 87).

Partners After All
Words and music by Chips Moman and Bobby Emmons.
Rightsong Music Inc., 1987/Chips Moman/Attadoo.
Introduced by Willie Nelson, from the album *Partners* (Columbia,
87).

Pink Cadillac
Revived in 1987 by Natalie Cole on the album *Everlasting*
(EMI-Manhattan, 87). For further details on this Springsteen
song, see *Popular Music, 1980-1984.*

The Pleasure Principle
Words and music by Monte Moir.
Flyte Tyme Tunes, 1986.
Best-selling record by Janet Jackson, from the album *Control* (A &
M, 86). This was the first single from Janet Jackson not to reach
the top ten; it was also the first not penned in part by her.

Point of No Return
Words and music by Lewis Martinee.
Panchin, 1985.
Best-selling record by Expose, from the album *Exposure* (Atlantic,
87). This song became a hit two years after its initial success in
the dance halls.

Privacy
Words and music by Craig Carnelia.

Frank Music Co., 1978.
Introduced off-Broadway in *The No-Frills Revue* (87).

Protect Yourself/My Nuts
Words and music by Damon Wimbley, Darren Robinson, Mark
  Morales, Jimmy Glenn, and Steve Linsley.
Missing Ball, 1987/Fat Boys.
Introduced by the Fat Boys on the popular sex therapy television
  show *Ask Dr. Ruth.* This rap describes the increasing sexual cau-
  tion among even the most macho element.

Putting Up with Me
Words and music by Mose Allison.
Audre Mae Music, 1987.
Introduced by Mose Allison on the album *Ever Since the World
  Ended* (Blue Note, 87). This song celebrates a marriage of long
  duration.

R

Radio Waves (English)
Words and music by Roger Waters.
Pink Floyd, London, England, 1987.
Best-selling record by Roger Waters, from the album *Radio K.A.O.S.* (Columbia, 87). Here the former member of Pink Floyd, now working a solo, once again took on the radio establishment.

Rain on You
Words and music by Phil Davis, Doug Erikson, and Butch Vig.
Flip 'n' Dog, 1987.
Introduced by Firetown on the album *In the Heart of the Heart Country* (Atlantic, 87). Co-author Butch Vig also owned the Madison, Wisconsin recording studio where the band recorded this album; he eventually became a member of the group as well.

Readin,' Rightin,' Route 23
Words and music by Dwight Yoakam.
Coal Dust West, 1987.
Introduced by Dwight Yoakam on the album *Hillbilly Deluxe* (Reprise, 87). The title comes from a phrase from the author's childhood that made fun of hillbillies.

Reality Row (English)
Words and music by Andy White.
Chappell & Co., Ltd., London, England, 1986.
Introduced by Andy White on the album *Rave On* (MCA, 86).

Rhythm Is Gonna Get You
Words and music by Gloria Estefan and Enrique Garcia.
Foreign Imported, 1987.
Best-selling record by Gloria Estefan and the Miami Sound Machine, from the album *Let It Loose* (Epic, 87).

Right Hand Man
Words and music by Gary Scruggs.
Earthly Delights, 1987.
Introduced by Eddy Raven on the album *Right Hand Man* (RCA, 87).

Right Next Door (Because of Me)
Words and music by Dennis Walker.
Calhoun Street, 1987.
Best-selling record by Robert Cray, from the album *Strong Persuader* (Hightone/Mercury, 87).

Right on Track
Words and music by Steve Bray and Steve Gilroy.
MCA Music, 1987/Unicity Music, Inc./Short Order.
Best-selling record by the Breakfast Club, from the album *The Breakfast Club* (MCA, 87). Bray, who has written many hits for Madonna, was originally a member of this band.

River of Fools
Words and music by David Hidalgo and Louie Perez.
Davince Music, 1987/No Ko Music.
Introduced by Los Lobos on the album *By the Light of the Moon* (Slash/Warner Bros., 87).

Rock Steady
Words and music by L.A. Babyface, D. Ladd, and B. Watson.
Hip-Trip Music Co., 1987/Hip Chic/Midstar Music, Inc./Hitwell.
Best-selling record by the Whispers, from the album *Just Gets Better with Time* (Solar, 87).

Romance
Words and music by Bill Berry, Peter Buck, Mike Mills, and Michael Stipe.
Night Garden Music, 1987/Unichappell Music Inc.
Introduced by R.E.M. in the film and album *Made in Heaven* (Elektra, 87).

Rose in Paradise
Words and music by Stewart Harris and Jim McBride.
Blackwood Music Inc., 1987/April Music, Inc.
Introduced by Waylon Jennings on the album *Hangin' Tough* (MCA, 87).

Running in the Family (English)
Words and music by Mark King, Wally Badarou, and Phil Gould.
Level 42 Songs, 1987/Chappell & Co., Inc./Island Visual Arts.

Best-selling record by Level 42, from the album *Running in the Family* (Polydor, 87).

S

Santa Baby
Revived in 1987 by Madonna on the album *A Very Special Christmas* (A & M). See *Popular Music, 1920-1979.*

Santa Claus Is Back in Town
Words and music by Jerry Leiber and Mike Stoller.
Elvis Presley Music, Inc., 1957, 1985/Rightsong Music Inc.
Performed by Dwight Yoakam (Reprise, 87).

Satellite
Words and music by Rob Hyman, Eric Bazilian, and Rick Chertoff.
Dub Notes, 1987/Human Boy Music/Hobbler Music.
Introduced by the Hooters on the album *One Way Home* (Columbia, 87). A lyric against television religion in the year of the downfall of Jim and Tammy Bakker.

Seasons Change
Words and music by Lewis Martinee.
Panchin, 1987/Screen Gems-EMI Music Inc.
Best-selling record by Expose, from the album *Exposure* (Arista, 87).

The Secret of My Success
Words and music by Jack Blades, David Foster, Tom Keane, and Mike Landau.
Music Corp. of America, 1987/MCA Music/Five Storks/Warner-Tamerlane Publishing Corp./Air Bear.
Introduced by Night Ranger as the title song for the film and soundtrack album of the same name (MCA, 87). Also included on the album *Big Life* by Night Ranger (MCA, 87). Nominated for a Golden Globe Award as Best Song from a Movie, 1987.

Set Me Free (Rosa Lee)
Words and music by Cesar Rosas.

Ceros, 1986.
Introduced by Los Lobos on the album *By the Light of the Moon* (Slash/Warner Bros., 87).

Seven Wonders
Words and music by Sandy Stewart and Stevie Nicks.
Welsh Witch Publishing, 1987.
Best-selling record by Fleetwood Mac, from the album *Tango in the Night* (Warner Bros., 87).

Shake Your Love
Words and music by Debbie Gibson.
Creative Bloc, 1987/Deborah Anne.
Best-selling record by Debbie Gibson, from the album *Out of the Blue* (Atlantic, 87).

Shakedown
Words and music by Harold Faltermeyer, Keith Forsey, and Bob Seger.
Famous Music Corp., 1987/Gear Publishing/Kilauea Music.
Introduced by Bob Seger in the film and on the soundtrack album *Beverly Hills Cop II* (MCA, 87). Best-selling record by Bob Seger. Nominated for a Golden Globe Award as Best Song from a Movie, 1987. Nominated for an Academy Award, Best Original Song, 1987.

She Was K.C. at Seven
Words and music by Craig Carnelia.
Introduced by Craig Carnelia in the Off-Broadway musical *Three Postcards* (87).

She's Like the Wind
Words and music by Patrick Swayze and Stacey Widelitz.
Troph, 1987.
Best-selling record by Patrick Swayze, with Wendy Fraser, from the soundtrack album *Dirty Dancing* (RCA, 87). Co-author Swayze was also one of the film's stars.

She's Too Good to Be True
Words and music by Sonny LeMaire and J. P. Pennington.
Tree Publishing Co., Inc., 1985/Pacific Island Music.
Best-selling record in 1987 by Exile, from their *Greatest Hits* album (Epic, 86).

Shine, Shine, Shine
Words and music by Bud McGuire and Ken Bell.
April Music, Inc., 1987/Butler's Bandits/Next o Ken/Ensign Music Corp.

Best-selling record by Eddy Raven, from the album *Right Hand Man* (RCA, 87).

Ship of Fools (Save Me from Tomorrow) (English)
Words and music by Karl Wallinger.
Bibo Music Publishers, 1986.
Best-selling record in 1987 by World Party, from the album *Private Revolution* (Chrysalis, 86).

Should've Known Better
Words and music by Richard Marx.
ChiBoy, 1987.
Best-selling record by Richard Marx, from the album *Richard Marx* (EMI-Manhattan, 87).

Show Me the Way
Words and music by Junior Potts, Joey Gallo, and Angela Winbush.
Almo Music Corp., 1987/He Gave Me.
Best-selling record by Regina Belle, from the album *All by Myself* (Columbia, 87).

Sign 'o' the Times
Words and music by Prince Rogers Nelson.
Dramatis Music Corp., 1987.
Best-selling record by Prince (Paisley Park, 87). Featured in the film and album of the same name.

Silent Night
Words by Joseph Mohr, music by Franz Gruber.
Revived in 1987 by Stevie Nicks on the album *A Very Special Christmas* (A & M). This holiday classic was written by an Austrian priest and a church organist in 1818.

Simple Things
Words and music by Jim Tullio and Allen Rubens.
Tools, 1985.
Introduced by by Richie Havens on the album *Simple Things* (RBI, 87).

Simply Meant to Be
Words by George Merrill and Shannon Rubicam, music by Henry Mancini.
TSP Music, Inc., 1987/Triple Star/Boy Meets Girl.
Introduced by Jennifer Warnes and Gary Morris on the soundtrack of the film *Blind Date* and on its album (Rhino, 87).

Sitting on a Fence (English)
Words and music by P. D. Heaton and Stan Cullimore.

Go! Discs Ltd., England, 1986.
Best-selling record by the Housemartins, from the album *London O Hull 4* (Elektra, 86). Melodic protest music from England.

Skeletons
Words and music by Stevie Wonder.
Jobete Music Co., Inc., 1987/Black Bull Music.
Best-selling record by Stevie Wonder, from the album *Characters* (Motown, 87). Nominated for a Grammy Award, Rhythm 'n' Blues Song of the Year, 1987.

Slow Down (English)
Words and music by Carl McIntosh, Steve Nichols, and Jane Eugene.
Brampton Music Ltd., England/MCA Music, 1986/Virgin Music, Inc.
Best-selling record in 1987 by Loose Ends, from the album *The Zagora* (MCA, 86).

Small Town Girl
Words and music by John Jarvis and Don Cook.
Tree Publishing Co., Inc., 1987/Cross Keys Publishing Co., Inc.
Best-selling record by Steve Wariner, from the album *It's a Crazy World* (MCA, 87).

Small Towns (Are Smaller for Girls)
Words and music by Mark Sanders, Alice Randall, and Verna Thompson.
Midsummer Music, 1987/AMR/April Music, Inc./Ides of March Music Division.
Introduced by Holly Dunn on the album *Cornerstone* (MTM, 87). The song offers an astute sociological commentary.

Smoking Gun
Words and music by D. Amy (pseudonym for Bruce Bromberg), Robert Cray, and Richard Cousins.
Calhoun Street, 1987/Bug Music/Robert Cray.
Best-selling record by Robert Cray, from the album *Strong Persuader* (Hightone/Mercury, 87); this was easily the bluesiest cut to enter the 1987 top forty.

Smooth Sailin' Tonight
Words and music by Angela Winbush.
Angel Notes, 1987/USA Exotica.
Best-selling record by the Isley Brothers, from the album *Smooth Sailin'* (Warner Bros., 87).

Snap Your Fingers
Revived in 1987 by Ronnie Milsap on the album *Heart and Soul* (RCA, 87). See *Popular Music, 1920-1979.*

So Different Now
Words and music by Felix Cavaliere and Michael Mugrage.
Largo Music, Inc., 1987.
Introduced by Felix Cavaliere on the soundtrack of the film *Hiding Out* and its album (Virgin, 87). Cavaliere was the lead vocalist of the popular 1960's group the Rascals.

So Emotional
Words and music by Billy Steinberg and Tom Kelly.
Billy Steinberg Music, 1987/Denise Barry Music.
Best-selling record by Whitney Houston, from her album *Whitney* (Arista, 87). One of 1987's hotter songwriting teams provided Houston with her sixth straight number-one song, equaling the record shared by the Beatles and the Bee Gees.

Somebody Lied
Words and music by J. Chambers and L. Jenkins.
Galleon Music, Inc., 1987.
Best-selling record by Ricky Van Shelton, from the album *Wild Eyed Dream* (Columbia, 87).

Someplace Else
Words and music by George Harrison.
Ganga Publishing Co., 1986/Zero Productions.
Revived in 1987 by George Harrison on the album *Cloud Nine* (Dark Horse, 87). Originally used in the Madonna film *Shanghai Surprise,* which Harrison produced.

Something in Your Eyes
Words and music by Richard Carpenter and Pamela Phillips Oland.
Almo Music Corp., 1987/Hammer & Nails Music/Irving Music Inc. /Pamalybo.
Introduced by Richard Carpenter and Dusty Springfield on the album *Time* (A & M, 87). The album marked Carpenter's first work since the death of his sister Karen, and provided one of two comeback showcases for classic British singer Springfield.

Something So Strong (Australian)
Words and music by Neil Finn and Mitchell Froom.
Roundhead, 1986/Wyoming Flesh.
Best-selling record in 1987 by Crowded House, from the album *Crowded House* (Chrysalis, 86).

Somewhere Down the Crazy River
Words and music by Robbie Robertson.
Medicine Hat Music, 1987.
Introduced by Robbie Robertson on the album *Robbie Robertson* (Geffen, 87). In this dramatic scenario, complete with monologue, the former member of the Band distills the essence of that group.

Somewhere Out There
See *Popular Music 1986.* Nominated for a Golden Globe Award as Best Song from a Movie in 1987. Won a Grammy Award, Song of the Year, 1987. Nominated for a Grammy Award, Best Song for TV Movie, 1987.

Somewhere Tonight
Words and music by Harlan Howard and Rodney Crowell.
Tree Publishing Co., Inc., 1987/Granite Music Corp./Coolwell Music.
Best-selling record by Highway 101, from the album *Highway 101* (Warner Bros., 87).

Songbird
Music by Kenny Gorlich.
Brenee, 1987.
Best-selling record by Kenny G., from the album *Duotones* (Arista, 87). This was the year's top instrumental.

Sorry Naomi
Words and music by Dan Stuart, Chris Cavacas, and Jack Waterson.
Dick James Music Inc., 1987.
Introduced by Green on Red on the album *The Killer Inside* (Mercury, 87). This song answers Naomi Judd of the country group the Judds, who made the song request "Grandpa (Tell Me About the Good Old Days)."

Spaceballs
Words and music by Jeffrey Pescetto, Clyde Lieberman, and Mel Brooks.
Colgems-EMI Music Inc., 1987/United Lion Music Inc.
Introduced by the Spinners on the soundtrack of the film *Spaceballs* and its album (Atlantic, 87).

Spare Parts
Words and music by Bruce Springsteen.
Bruce Springsteen Publishing, 1987.
Introduced by Bruce Springsteen on the album *Tunnel of Love* (Columbia, 87).

Starlight Express (English)
Music by Andrew Lloyd Webber, words by Richard Stilgoe.
The Really Useful Group, England, 1987.
Introduced by Greg Mowry in the 1987 Broadway production of
Starlight Express, but was included in the earlier production in
England. Also performed by El DeBarge on the album *Music and
Songs from "Starlight Express"* (MCA, 87).

Still a Thrill
Words and music by Andre Cymone and Jody Watley.
Ultrawave, 1987/April Music, Inc./Rightsong Music Inc.
Best-selling record by Jody Watley, from the album *Jody Watley*
(MCA, 87).

Still of the Night (English)
Words and music by David Coverdale and John Sykes.
Whitesnake, 1987/WB Music Corp.
Best-selling record by Whitesnake, from the album *Whitesnake*
(Geffen, 87), this number recalls the heyday of Led Zeppelin.

Still Waiting
Words and music by Prince Rogers Nelson.
Controversy Music, 1987.
Introduced by Rainy Davis on the album *Sweetheart* (Columbia,
87).

Stone Love
Words and music by Charles Smith and James Taylor, words and
music by Kool and the Gang.
Delightful Music Ltd., 1986.
Best-selling record in 1987 by Kool and the Gang, from the album
Forever (Mercury, 86).

Stood Up
Words and music by John Hiatt.
Lillybilly, 1987.
Introduced by John Hiatt on the album *Bring the Family* (A & M,
87).

Stop to Love
Words and music by Luther Vandross and Nat Adderly, Jr.
April Music, Inc., 1987/Uncle Ronnie's Music Co., Inc./Dillard.
Best-selling record in 1987 by Luther Vandross from the album
Give Me the Reason (Epic, 86).

Storybook Love
Words and music by Willy DeVille.

Crosstown, 1987.
Introduced by Willy DeVille on the soundtrack of the film *The Princess Bride* and on its album (Warner Bros., 87). Nominated for an Academy Award, Best Original Song, 1987.

Straight to the Heart
Words and music by Graham Lyle and Terry Britten.
Irving Music Inc., 1986/Chappell & Co., Inc.
Best-selling record in 1987 by Crystal Gayle, from the album *Straight to the Heart* (Warner Bros., 86).

Strange Weather
Words and music by Tom Waits and Kathleen Brennan.
Jalma, 1987.
Introduced by Marianne Faithfull on the album *Strange Weather* (Island, 87). This cut offered one of 1987's more perfect marriages of writer and song, with Waits and Faithfull a couple of rare birds of the same ruffled feather. Kathleen Brennan is the wife of co-author Tom Waits.

The Stuff That Dreams Are Made Of
Words and music by Carly Simon.
C'est Music, 1987.
Introduced by Carly Simon on the album *Coming Around Again* (Arista, 86); the album's title proved prophetic considering Simon's remarkable comeback in 1987.

Sue Lee
Words and music by Willie Nile and Rick Chertoff.
River House, 1986/Hobbler Music.
Introduced by Patty Smyth on the album *Never Enough* (Columbia, 87).

Summer Wages (Canadian)
Words and music by Ian Tyson.
WB Music Corp., 1987.
Introduced by Ian Tyson on the album *Cowboyography* (Sugar Hill, 87).

Summer's Cauldron (English)
Words and music by Andy Partridge.
Virgin Nymph, 1986/Virgin Music Ltd.
Introduced by XTC on the album *Skylarking* (Geffen, 87).

Surfin' Bird
Revived in 1987 by Pee Wee Herman in the movie and on the soundtrack album *Back to the Beach* (Columbia, 87). See *Popular Music, 1920-1979.*

Sweet Fire of Love
Words and music by Robbie Robertson, words and music by U2.
Medicine Hat Music, 1987/U2/Chappell & Co., Inc.
Introduced by Robbie Robertson on the album *Robbie Robertson* (Geffen, 87).

Sweet Kentucky Ham
Words and music by David Frishberg.
Swiftwater Music, 1987.
Performed by David Fishberg on the album *Can't Take You Nowhere* (Fantasy, 87). Fishberg follows in the Mose Allison tradition of supper club blues singing.

Sweet Sixteen
Words and music by Billy Idol.
Boneidol Music, 1986/Rare Blue Music, Inc.
Best-selling record in 1987 by Billy Idol, from the album *Whiplash Smile* (Chrysalis, 86).

System of Survival
Words and music by Skylark.
Sputnick Adventure, 1987/Maurice White.
Best-selling record by Earth, Wind, and Fire, from the album *Touch the World* (Columbia, 87).

T

Talk Dirty to Me
Words and music by Bobby Dall, C. C. DeVille, Brett Michaels, and Rikki Rocket.
Sweet Cyanide, 1986.
Best-selling record in 1987 by Poison, from the album *Look What the Cat Dragged In* (Enigma, 86).

Tearing Us Apart (English)
Words and music by Eric Clapton and Greg Phillinganes.
E.C. Music, England, 1986/Poopys.
Best-selling record in 1987 by Eric Clapton, from the album *August* (Duck/Warner Bros., 86).

Telepathy
Words and music by J. Coco (pseudonym for Prince Rogers Nelson).
Controversy Music, 1987.
Introduced by Deborah Allen on the album *Telepathy* (RCA, 87).

Tell It to My Heart
Words and music by Seth Swirsky and Ernie Gold.
Chappell & Co., Inc., 1987/November Nights/Goldpoint.
Best-selling record by Taylor Dayne, from the album *Tell It to My Heart* (Arista, 87).

Telling Me Lies (English)
Words and music by Linda Thompson and Betsy Cook.
Firesign Music Ltd., England/Chappell & Co., Inc., 1985.
Revived in 1986 by Dolly Parton, Emmylou Harris, and Linda Ronstadt on the album *Trio* (Warner Bros.). Linda Thompson had introduced the song on her earlier Warner Bros. album, *Can't Stop the Girl.* Nominated for a Grammy Award, Country Song of the Year, 1987.

That Ain't Love
Words and music by Kevin Cronin.
Fate Music, 1987.
Best-selling record by Reo Speedwagon on the album *Life As We Know It* (Epic, 87).

That Was a Close One
Words and music by Robert Byrne.
Rick Hall Music, 1987.
Introduced by Earl Thomas Conley on the album *Too Many Times* (RCA, 87).

That's What Love Is All About
Words and music by Michael Bolton and Eric Kaz.
Emboe, 1987/Kaz Music Co./April Music, Inc.
Best-selling record by Michael Bolton, from the album *The Hunger* (Columbia, 87). This was the breakthrough song for the journeyman singer-songwriter.

(I've Had) The Time of My Life
Words and music by Franke Preurte, John DeNicola, and Donald Markowitz.
Knockout Music Co., 1987/Jemava/Donald Jay/R.U. Cerious.
Best-selling record by Bill Medley and Jennifer Warnes, from the hit film and soundtrack album *Dirty Dancing* (RCA, 87). This big ballad from the year's most successful soundtrack album won the 1987 Academy Award as Best Original Song, a Golden Globe Award as Best Song from a Movie, and was nominated for a Grammy Award, 1987, as Best Song for a Movie/TV.

Then It's Love
Words and music by Dennis Linde.
Dennis Linde Music, 1987.
Best-selling record by Don Williams (Capital, 87).

There's a Light beyond These Woods (Mary Margaret)
Words and music by Nanci Griffith.
Wing & Wheel, 1978, 1982, 1986.
Revived in 1986 by Nanci Griffith on the album *Lone Star State of Mind* (MCA). Griffith originally recorded the song on her 1978 album that was named after it (Philo).

There's Nothing Better than Love
Words and music by Luther Vandross and J. Skip Anderson.
April Music, Inc., 1987/Uncle Ronnie's Music Co., Inc./JVA.
Best-selling record by Luther Vandross and Gregory Hines, from the album *Give Me the Reason* (Spic, 87).

There's the Girl
Words and music by Holly Knight and Nancy Wilson.
Makiki Publishing Co., Ltd., 1987/Knighty Knight/Know Music/
Arista Music, Inc.
Best-selling record by Heart, from the album *Bad Animals* (Capitol,
87).

They Dance Alone (English)
Words and music by Sting (pseudonym for Gordon Sumner).
Magnetic, England, 1987/Reggatta Music, Ltd./Illegal Songs, Inc.
Introduced by Sting on the album *Nothing Like the Sun* (A & M);
this song typifies the artist's haunting brand of social protest.

This Crazy Love
Words and music by Roger Murrah and J. Hicks.
Tom Collins Music Corp., 1987.
Best-selling record by the Oak Ridge Boys, from the album *Where
the Fast Love Ends* (RCA, 87).

This Girl's Back in Town
Words and music by Paul Jabara and Bob Esty.
Poperetta, 1987/Warner-Tamerlane Publishing Corp./Fave Rave.
Introduced by Raquel Welch on her home video exercise tape *A
Week with Raquel/7-Day Wake Up and Shape Up* (Total Video,
87). Also released as a twelve-inch single for the dance and aero-
bics market (Columbia, 87).

This Is the Time
Best-selling record by Billy Joel (Columbia, 87). See *Popular Music
1986.*

Three-Legged Man
Words and music by Shel Silverstein.
TRO-Hollis Music, Inc., 1987.
Introduced by Ray Stevens on the album *Cracking Up* (MCA, 87).

Three Time Loser
Words and music by Dan Seals.
Pink Pig Music, 1986.
Best-selling record in 1987 by Dan Seals, from the album *On the
Front Line* (EMI-America, 86).

A Time for Heroes
Words and music by Jon Lyons, M. Scott Sotebeer, and Rik
Emmett.
Little Horn Music.
Introduced by Meat Loaf, with Brian May of Queen on guitar (Or-
pheum, 87); the song was also recorded by the instrumental group

Tangerine Dream. Legal complications prevented this from being used as a theme for the International Special Olympics, as originally was intended.

Time Out for the Burglar
Words and music by Pamela Phillips Oland, Randy Jackson, Jackie Jackson, Bernard Edwards, Robert Hart, Tony Thompson, Eddie Martinez, and Jeff Bova.
Irving Music Inc., 1987/Yonder/Yiggy/Ransaca.
Introduced by the Jacksons on the soundtrack of the film *Burglar* and its album (MCA, 87).

To Know Him Is to Love Him
Revived in 1986 by Dolly Parton, Emmylou Harris, and Linda Ronstadt on the album *Trio* (Warner Bros.). Phil Spector wrote the song in 1958 as an epitaph for his father and it has been revived several times over the years; see *Popular Music, 1920-1979.*

Tonight, Tonight, Tonight (English)
Words and music by Anthony Banks, Phil Collins, and Mike Rutherford.
Anthony Banks, England, 1987/Phil Collins, England/Mike Rutherford, England/Hit & Run Music.
Best-selling record in 1987 by Genesis, from the album *Invisible Touch* (Atlantic, 86). Television exposure as theme music in a Michelob beer commercial helped make this a hit.

Touch Me (I Want Your Body) (English)
Words and music by M. Shreeve, J. Astrop, and P. Q. Harris.
Zomba Enterprises, Inc., 1987.
Best-selling record in 1987 by Samantha Fox, from the album *Touch Me* (Jive, 86).

Touch of Grey
Words by Robert Hunter, music by Jerry Garcia.
Ice Nine Publishing Co., Inc., 1987.
Best-selling record by the Grateful Dead, from the album *In the Dark* (Arista, 87). This hit marked a major comeback for the ageless San Francisco band.

Trail of Broken Treaties
Words and music by Steve Van Zant.
Little Steven Music, 1986.
Introduced by Little Steven on the album *Freedom--No Compromise* (Manhattan, 86); another expression of political rock from the former Bruce Springsteen sideman.

Trouble in the Fields
Words and music by Nanci Griffith and Rick West.
Wing & Wheel.
Introduced by Nanci Griffith on the album *Lone Star State of Mind* (MCA, 86); here the singer-songwriter addresses the concerns of farmers.

Tunnel of Love
Words and music by Bruce Springsteen.
Bruce Springsteen Publishing, 1987.
Best-selling record by Bruce Springsteen, from the album *Tunnel of Love* (Columbia, 87); the author-performer provides a metaphor for the marital experience.

Twelve Rough Years
Words and music by Elizabeth Swados.
Blackwood Music Inc., 1987.
Introduced by Ashanti Isabell in the 1987 musical *Swing.*

Twenty Years Ago
Words and music by Michael Spriggs, Wood Newton, Daniel Tyler, and Michael Noble.
Warner House of Music, 1987/WB Gold Music Corp.
Best-selling record by Kenny Rogers, from the album *They Don't Make Them Like They Used To* (RCA).

U-V

U Got the Look
Words and music by Prince Rogers Nelson.
Controversy Music, 1987.
Best-selling record by Prince, from the album and movie soundtrack *Sign 'o' the Times* (Paisley Park, 87). Nominated for a Grammy Award, Rhythm 'n' Blues Song of the Year, 1987.

Under the Boardwalk
Revived in 1986 by Bruce Willis on the album *The Return of Bruno* (Motown), which featured the star of television's *Moonlighting* as a mythical rock 'n' roller. See *Popular Music, 1920-1979.*

Up the Ladder to the Roof
Revived in 1987 by John Kydd (Nightwave, 87), whose back-up singers included former Supremes Cindy Birdsong, Lynda Lawrence, and Scherrie Payne. The Supremes had a hit with this song in 1970; see *Popular Music, 1920-1979.*

Valentine's Day
Words and music by Bruce Springsteen.
Bruce Springsteen Publishing, 1987.
Introduced by Bruce Springsteen on the album *Tunnel of Love* (Columbia, 87).

Valerie
Words by Will Jennings, music by Steve Winwood.
Island Music, 1982/Blue Sky Rider Songs/Willin' David.
Revived in 1987 by Steve Winwood on the album *Chronicle* (Island); Winwood originally used the song on the album *Talking Back to the Night.*

Vanna, Pick Me a Letter, also known as **The Letter**
Introduced by Dr. Dave on the album *Dr. Dave* (TSR, 87). This tribute to Vanna White, the hostess on the television game show

Wheel of Fortune , is set to the music for the Box Tops' 1967 hit, "The Letter"; see *Popular Music, 1920-1979.* The new lyrics by Dave Kolin and Wayne Carson Thompson were registered for copyright in 1986.

Verdi Cries
Words and music by Natalie Merchant.
Christian Burial, 1987.
Introduced by 10,000 Maniacs on the album *In My Tribe* (Elektra, 87).

W

Walk Like a Man
Words and music by Bruce Springsteen.
Bruce Springsteen Publishing, 1987.
Introduced by Bruce Springsteen on the album *Tunnel of Love* (Columbia, 87).

Walk with an Erection
Words by Liam Sternberg and Johnny Angel, music by Liam Sternberg.
Peer International Corp.
Performed by the Swinging Erudites (Airwave, 87); this lewd parody of the 1986 Bangles' hit, "Walk like an Egyptian," was denied license by copyright holders, but it became an underground hit nonetheless.

Wanted Dead or Alive
Words and music by Jon Bon Jovi and Richie Sambora.
Bon Jovi Publishing, 1986/Polygram Music Publishing Inc.
Best-selling record in 1987, from the album *Slippery When Wet* (Polygram, 86).

The Way We Make a Broken Heart
Words and music by John Hiatt.
Bug Music, 1981/Bilt.
Best-selling record by Rosanne Cash, from the album *King's Record Store* (Columbia, 87). Introduced by Ry Cooder on the album *Borderline* (Warner Bros., 80).

The Way You Make Me Feel
Words and music by Michael Jackson.
Mijac Music, 1987/Warner-Tamerlane Publishing Corp.
Best-selling record by Michael Jackson, from the album *Bad* (Epic, 87).

We Want Some Pussy
Words and music by Luther Campbell.
Introduced by 2 Live Crew on the album *2 Live Crew Is What We Are* (Luke Skywalker Records, 87). This song and album led to the arrest of a salesgirl in Florida for distributing lewd material to minors. Charges were later dropped.

The Weekend
Words and music by Bill La Bounty and Brent Maher.
Screen Gems-EMI Music Inc., 1987.
Best-selling record by Steve Wariner, from the album *It's a Crazy World* (MCA, 87).

We'll Be Together (English)
Words and music by Sting (pseudonym for Gordon Sumner).
Magnetic, England, 1987/Reggatta Music, Ltd./Illegal Songs, Inc./ Atlantic Music Corp.
Best-selling record by Sting, from the album *Nothing Like the Sun* (A & M, 87).

We're Ready
Words and music by Tom Scholz.
Hideaway Hits, 1987.
Best-selling record in 1987 by Boston, from the album *Third Stage* (MCA, 86). This song's title seems ironic considering the seven years Scholz spent producing the group's third album.

West LA Fadeaway
Words and music by Jerry Garcia and Robert Hunter.
Ice Nine Publishing Co., Inc., 1984.
Introduced by the Grateful Dead on the album *In the Dark* (Arista, 87).

We've Never Danced
Words and music by Neil Young.
Silver Fiddle/Marilor Music.
Introduced by Martha Davis on the soundtrack of the film *Made in Heaven* and its album (Elektra, 87).

We've Only Just Begun (The Romance Is Not Over)
Words and music by Timmy Allen and Glenn Jones.
Willesden Music, Inc., 1987/Lu Ella.
Best-selling record by Glenn Jones, from the album *Glenn Jones* (Jive, 87).

What Are We Making Weapons For, also known as **Let Us Begin,**
Words and music by John Denver.
Cherry Mountain, 1986.

Introduced by John Denver and Soviet singer Alexandre Gradsky
in a recording for release in the United Stated by RCA and in the
Soviet Union by Melodiya. The song, which protests the arms
race, is on Denver's album *One World* (RCA, 86).

What Have I Done to Deserve This (English)
Words and music by Neil Tennant, Chris Lowe, and Allee Willis.
Cage, England, 1987/10 Music Ltd., England/Texas City/
Streamline Moderne.
Best-selling record by the Pet Shop Boys and Dusty Springfield,
from the album *Actually* (EMI, 87). The veteran English soul
singer joined younger colleagues for the second time in 1987 with
this record.

What You Get Is What You See (English)
Words and music by Terry Britten and Graham Lyle.
Myake, England, 1986/WB Music Corp./Almo Music Corp.
Best-selling record in 1987 by Tina Turner, from the album *Break
Every Rule* (Capitol, 86).

What's Going On
Revived in 1986 by Cyndi Lauper on the album *True Colors*
(Portrait). See *Popular Music, 1920-1979.*

What's My Scene (Australian)
Words and music by Dave Faulkner.
Copyright Control, 1987.
Introduced by the Hoodoo Gurus on the album *Blow Your Cool*
(Elektra, 87).

When Smokey Sings (English)
Words and music by Martin Fry and Mark White.
Virgin Nymph, 1987.
Best-selling record by ABC, from the album *ABC in Alphabet City*
(Mercury, 87). This song occupied the same top ten as Smokey
Robinson's own comeback single.

Where Did I Go Wrong
Words and music by Joe Raposo.
Jonico Music Inc., 1987.
Introduced in the Connecticut production of the musical *The Little
Rascals.*

Where the Streets Have No Name (Irish)
Words and music by U2.
Chappell & Co., Inc., 1987/U2.
Best-selling record by U2, from the album *The Joshua Tree* (Island,
87). This song packs an emotionally searing message.

Whiskey, If You Were a Woman
Words and music by Mary Francis, Johnny Macrae, and Bob Morrison.
Southern Nights Music Co., 1987.
Best-selling record by Highway 101, from the album *Highway 101* (Warner Bros., 87).

White Rabbit
Revived in 1986 by the Jefferson Starship on the soundtrack of the film *Platoon* and on its album (Atlantic, 86). The twentieth anniversary of the "Summer of Love---1968--when this song was first on the charts, boosted its revival. It was also used on the Jefferson Airplane retrospective collection *2400 Fulton Street* (RCA, 87). See *Popular Music, 1920-1979.*

Who Found Who
Words and music by Paul Gurvitz.
Rare Blue Music, Inc., 1987.
Best-selling record by Elisa Fiorello and Jellybean Benitez, from the album *Who Found Who* (Chrysalis). Benitez, previously a DJ at the New York City disco Studio 54, discovered singer Elisa Fiorello on the television contest *Star Search.*

Who Will You Run To
Words and music by Diane Warren.
Realsongs, 1987.
Best-selling record by Heart, from the album *Bad Animals* (Capitol, 87).

Who's That Girl
Words and music by Madonna and Patrick Leonard.
WB Music Corp., 1987/Bleu Disque Music/Webo Girl Music/WB Music Corp./Johnny Yuma.
Introduced by Madonna in the film and on the soundtrack album *Who's That Girl* (Sire, 87). When this song reached the top five, Madonna's twelfth single in a row to do so, she needed just three more such hits to overtake the Beatles or twelve more to tie Elvis Presley for the longest string of chart-toppers. Nominated for a Grammy Award, Song for TV/Movie, 1987.

Why Does It Have to Be (Wrong or Right)
Words and music by Randy Sharp and Donny Lowery.
Warner-Tamerlane Publishing Corp., 1987/Rumble Seat/Sheddhouse Music.
Best-selling record by Restless Heart, from the album *Wheels* (RCA, 87).

Why You Treat Me So Bad
Words and music by Jay King, Thom McElroy, and David Foster.
Jay King, IV, 1987.
Best-selling record by Club Nouveau, from the album *Life, Love, and Pain* (Tommy Boy, 87).

Will You Still Love Me
Words and music by David Foster, Tom Keane, and Richard Baskin.
Air Bear, 1986/Warner-Tamerlane Publishing Corp./Music Corp. of America/Young Millionaires Club/Warner Springs.
Best-selling record in 1987 by Chicago, from the album *Chicago 18* (Warner Bros., 86).

Winner Takes All
Words and music by Giorgio Moroder and Tom Whitlock.
GMPC, 1987/Go Glow.
Introduced by Sammy Hagar in the film and on the soundtrack album *Over the Top* (Columbia, 87). Best-selling record by Hagar.

Winter Wonderland
Revived in 1987 by Eurhythmics on the album *A Very Special Christmas* (A & M). See *Popular Music, 1920-1979.*

Wipe Out
Revived in 1987 by the Fat Boys and the Beach Boys in the film *Disorderlies* and its soundtrack album (Tin Pan Apple/Polygram, 87). See *Popular Music, 1920-1979.*

With or without You (Irish)
Words and music by U2.
Chappell & Co., Inc., 1987/U2.
Best-selling record in 1987 by U2, from the album *The Joshua Tree* (Island, 87). This was the first hit single from the album band of the year.

World Where You Live (Australian)
Words and music by Neil Finn.
Roundhead, 1986.
Introduced by Crowded House on the album *Crowded House* (Chrysalis, 86).

Wot's It to Ya
Words and music by Robbie Nevil and Broek Walsh.
MCA Music, 1986.
Best-selling record by Robbie Nevil, from the album *Robbie Nevil* (Manhattan, 86).

Would Jesus Wear a Rolex
Words and music by Chet Atkins and Margaret Archer.
Leona, 1987.
Introduced by Ray Stevens on the album *Crackin' Up* (MCA, 87).
  Although the song was written previously, it was ready to capital-
  ize on this year's contretemps in the realms of television evangel-
  ism.

Y

You Again
Words and music by Don Schlitz and Paul Overstreet.
MCA Music, 1987/Don Schlitz Music/Writer's Group Music/
  Scarlet Moon Music.
Best-selling record by the Forester Sisters, from the album *You
  Again* (Warner Bros., 87).

You and Me Tonight
Words and music by Eban Kelly, Jimi Randolph, and K. Moore.
Virgin Nymph, 1987/Attractive.
Best-selling record by Deja, from the album *Serious* (Virgin, 87).

You Are the Girl
Words and music by Ric Ocasek.
Lido Music Inc., 1987.
Best-selling record by the Cars, from the album *Door to Door*
  (Elektra, 87).

You Don't Own Me
Revived in 1987 by the Blow Monkeys, on the soundtrack of the
  film *Dirty Dancing* and its album (RCA, 87). This version trans-
  mogrified the Lesley Gore classic. See *Popular Music, 1920-1979.*

You Got It All
Words and music by Rupert Holmes.
Holmes Line of Music, 1986.
Best-selling record in 1987 by the Jets, from the album *The Jets*
  (MCA, 86). With this release, songwriter Holmes moved back to
  the charts from Broadway, where his *Mystery of Edwin Drood* was
  a big success.

You Got Me Floating
Words and music by Jimi Hendrix.
Bella Godiva Music.

Revived in 1987 by Joan Jett and the Blackhearts on the album *Good Music* (Blackheart/CBS, 86).

You Keep Me Hanging On
Revived in 1987 by Kim Wilde on the album *Another Step* (MCA). This was the third time the song reached the top ten, the Supremes and Vanilla Fudge having previously taken it there. See *Popular Music, 1920-1979.*

You Make Me Want to Love Again
Words and music by Leon Ware and Billy Valentine.
Bibo Music Publishers, 1987/Welk Music Group/William V.
Introduced by Vesta Williams on the album *Vesta* (A & M, 87).

You Still Move Me
Words and music by Dan Seals.
Pink Pig Music, 1986.
Best-selling record in 1987 by Dan Seals, from the album *On the Front Line* (EMI-America, 86).

You Win Again (English)
Words and music by Barry Gibb, Robin Gibb, and Maurice Gibb.
Gibb Brothers Music, 1987/Unichappell Music Inc.
Introduced by the Bee Gees on the album *E.S.P.* (Warner Bros., 87).

Your Dad Did
Words and music by John Hiatt.
Lillybilly, 1987.
Introduced by John Hiatt, from the album *Bring the Family* (A & M, 87).

You're My First Lady
Words and music by Mac McAnally.
Beginner Music, 1987.
Best-selling record by T. G. Sheppard, from the album *It Still Rains in Memphis* (Columbia, 87).

You're Never Too Old for Young Love
Words and music by Rick Giles and Frank Myers.
Colgems-EMI Music Inc., 1987.
Best-selling record by Eddy Raven, from the album *Right Hand Man* (RCA, 87).

"You've Got" The Touch
Words and music by Will Robinson, John Jarrard, and Lisa Palas.
Alabama Band Music Co.
Best-selling record in 1987 by Alabama, from the album *The Touch* (MCA, 86).

Indexes and List of Publishers

Lyricists & Composers Index

Adams, Bryan
  Back to Paradise
  Hearts on Fire
  Heat of the Night
Adams, Terry
  I Want You Bad
Adderly, Nat, Jr.
  Stop to Love
Afanasieff, W.
  Don't Make Me Wait for Love
Aitken, Matt
  I Heard a Rumour
Alger, Patrick
  Lone Star State of Mind
Allen, Timmy
  I'm in Love
  (You're Puttin') A Rush on Me
  We've Only Just Begun (The
    Romance Is Not Over)
Allison, Mose
  Ever Since the World Ended
  I Looked in the Mirror
  Putting Up with Me
Alvin, Dave
  Fourth of July
Amy, D.
  Smoking Gun
Anderson, J. Skip
  There's Nothing Better than Love
Anderson, Terry
  Battleship Chains

Andrews, Reginald
  Let's Wait Awhile
Angel, Johnny
  Walk with an Erection
Anka, Paul
  Leave It All to Me
  No Way Out
Archer, Margaret
  Would Jesus Wear a Rolex
Aston, Jon
  Heartbreak Beat
Astrop, J.
  Touch Me (I Want Your Body)
Atkins, Chet
  Would Jesus Wear a Rolex
Aykroyd, Dan
  City of Crime
Aykroyd, Peter
  City of Crime
Babyface, L.A.
  Rock Steady
Bacharach, Burt
  Everchanging Times
  Love Power
Badarou, Wally
  Lessons in Love
  Running in the Family
Bailey, Chris
  Just Like Fire Would
Bakker, Tammy Faye
  The Ballad of Jim and Tammy

Lyricists & Composers Index

Coco, J.
  Telepathy
Cody, Phil
  Doing It All for My Baby
Coffey, Charlie
  The Homecoming Queen's Got a
  Gun
  I Like 'Em Big and Stupid
Cohen, Douglas J.
  I've Noticed a Change
Cohen, Jeffrey
  Jimmy Lee
Cohen, Leonard
  Ain't No Cure for Love
  First We Take Manhattan
Colcord, Ray
  The Homecoming Queen's Got a
  Gun
  I Like 'Em Big and Stupid
Colker, Jerry
  Crazy World
  It's Getting Harder to Love You
Collen, Phil
  Animal
Collins, Phil
  In Too Deep
  Tonight, Tonight, Tonight
Colton, Tony
  I'm No Angel
Conley, David
  Happy
Conley, Earl Thomas
  I Need a Good Woman Bad
Conti, Bill
  Everchanging Times
Cook, Betsy
  Telling Me Lies
Cook, Don
  Julia
  Small Town Girl
Cooler, Whey
  Catch Me (I'm Falling)
Cope, Laforest
  see La La
Coverdale, David
  Here I Go Again
  In This Love
  Still of the Night

Coy, Steven
  Brand New Lover
Craver, Mike
  Ohio Afternoon
Cray, Robert
  Bad Influence
  Smoking Gun
Cronin, Kevin
  In My Dreams
  That Ain't Love
Crowell, Rodney
  Somewhere Tonight
Cullimore, Stan
  Happy Hour
  Sitting on a Fence
Cymone, Andre
  Looking for a New Love
  Still a Thrill
Dall, Bobby
  I Won't Forget You
  Talk Dirty to Me
Dallin, Sarah
  I Heard a Rumour
Davis, Paul
  Carry the Torch
  Heart Country
  Love Me Like You Used To
Davis, Phil
  Rain on You
Dean, Steve
  It Takes a Little Rain
DeBurgh, Chris
  The Lady in Red
Decker, Carol
  Heart and Soul
Delp, Brad
  Can'tcha Say (You Believe in Me)
DeNicola, John
  (I've Had) The Time of My Life
Denver, John
  What Are We Making Weapons
  For
Deville, C. C.
  I Won't Forget You
DeVille, C. C.
  Talk Dirty to Me
DeVille, Willy
  Storybook Love

Dewese, Moe
  Go See the Doctor
Difford, Chris
  Hourglass
Dillon, Dean
  Ocean Front Property
Duke, M.
  Doing It All for My Baby
Dunn, Holly
  Love Someone Like Me
Dylan, Bob
  Gotta Serve Somebody
  Had a Dream About You, Baby
  Jammin' Me
  Night After Night
Earle, Steve
  I Ain't Ever Satisfied
  My Baby Worships Me
  Nowhere Road
Eastman, Barry
  Dominoes
Eastmond, Barry
  Have You Ever Loved Somebody
Ebb, Fred
  The Kid Herself
Edmonds, Kenny
  I'd Still Say Yes
Edwards, Bernard
  Time Out for the Burglar
Eede, Nick
  (I Just) Died in Your Arms
  I've Been in Love Before
Elliott, Jack
  I'm Not Ashamed to Cry
Emmett, Rik
  A Time for Heroes
Emmons, Bobby
  Love Me Like You Used To
  Partners After All
Erikson, Doug
  Carry the Torch
  Heart Country
  Rain on You
Erving, B.
  I Need Love
Escovedo, Sheila
  Hold Me

Estefan, Gloria
  Rhythm Is Gonna Get You
Esty, Bob
  This Girl's Back in Town
Etts, S.
  I Need Love
Eugene, Jane
  Slow Down
Ezrin, Bob
  Learning to Fly
Fahey, Siobhan
  I Heard a Rumour
Faltermeyer, Harold
  Shakedown
Farriss, Andrew
  Need You Tonight
Faulkner, Dave
  Good Times
  In the Middle of the Land
  Out That Door
  What's My Scene
Feldman, Jack
  Let Freedom Ring
Feliciato, Phil
  see Cody, Phil
Fenton, George
  Cry Freedom
Finn, Neil
  Don't Dream It's Over
  Something So Strong
  World Where You Live
Forrest, George
  The Broken Pianolita
Forsey, Keith
  Shakedown
Foster, David
  Love Lights the World
    (Rendezvous)
  The Secret of My Success
  Why You Treat Me So Bad
  Will You Still Love Me
Foster, G.
  Love Is a House
Foster, Radney
  Love Someone Like Me
Franceschi, Kendall
  Love, You Ain't Seen the Last of
    Me

Lyricists & Composers Index

Francis, Mary
  Whiskey, If You Were a Woman
Frank, David
  Don't Disturb This Groove
Frishberg, David
  Green Hills of Earth
  Sweet Kentucky Ham
Froom, Mitchell
  Something So Strong
Fry, Martin
  When Smokey Sings
Full Force
  Head to Toe
  Lost in Emotion
  (If You) Love Me Just a Little
Gabriel, Peter
  Big Time
  Biko
  Don't Give Up
Gaitsch, Bruce
  Boys Night Out
  Don't Mean Nothin
  La Isla Bonita
Galdston, Phil
  It's Not Over ('Til It's Over)
Gallo, Joey
  Show Me the Way
Gamble, Kenny
  Lovin' You
Garcia, Enrique
  Rhythm Is Gonna Get You
Garcia, Jerry
  Touch of Grey
  West LA Fadeaway
George, Jimmy
  I Wonder Who She's Seeing Now
  Just to See Her
Gershwin, George
  Lonely Boy
Gibb, Barry
  You Win Again
Gibb, Maurice
  You Win Again
Gibb, Robin
  You Win Again
Gibson, Debbie
  Only in My Dreams
  Shake Your Love

Giles, Rick
  You're Never Too Old for Young
    Love
Gilmour, David
  Learning to Fly
Gilroy, Steve
  Right on Track
Giraldo,
  Back to Paradise
Glass, Preston
  Don't Make Me Wait for Love
  Jimmy Lee
Glenn, Jimmy
  Protect Yourself/My Nuts
Gold, Ernie
  Tell It to My Heart
Gold, Julie
  From a Distance
Golde, Franne
  Be There
  Don't You Want Me
Goldmark, Andy
  Flames of Paradise
Goodrum, Randy
  If She Would Have Been Faithful
Gordon, Marc
  My Forever Love
Gorlich, Kenny
  Songbird
Gould, Phil
  Lessons in Love
  Running in the Family
Gramm, Lou
  Midnight Blue
Green, J.
  Can'tcha Say (You Believe in Me)
Greenwich, Ellie
  Christmas (Baby Please Come
    Home)
Griffith, Nanci
  Beacon Street
  Cold Hearts/Closed Minds
  Ford Econoline
  There's a Light beyond These
    Woods (Mary Margaret)
  Trouble in the Fields
Gruber, Franz
  Silent Night

134

Lyricists & Composers Index

Jackson, Freddie
  Jam Tonight
Jackson, Jackie
  Time Out for the Burglar
Jackson, Janet
  Let's Wait Awhile
Jackson, Marlon
  Don't Go
Jackson, Michael
  Bad
  I Can't Stop Loving You
  The Way You Make Me Feel
Jackson, Randy
  Time Out for the Burglar
Jagger, Mick
  Let's Work
Jam, Jimmy
  Diamonds
  Fake
  Just the Facts
Jarrard, John
  –You've Got" The Touch
Jarvis, John
  Julia
  Small Town Girl
Jenkins, L.
  Somebody Lied
Jenkins, Tomi
  Back and Forth
  Candy
Jenner, Linda Thompson
  Love Lights the World
    (Rendezvous)
Jennings, Will
  Back in the High Life Again
  Boys Night Out
  Didn't We Almost Have It All
  The Finer Things
  Love Lives On
  Valerie
John, Elton
  Candle in the Wind
Jones, Bucky
  Fewer Threads than These
Jones, David Lynn
  Bonnie Jean (Little Sister)
  Living in the Promiseland

Jones, Glenn
  We've Only Just Begun (The
    Romance Is Not Over)
K., Tonio
  I'm Supposed to Have Sex with
    You
Kamen, Michael
  Lethal Weapon
Kander, John
  The Kid Herself
Kane, Kieran
  Can't Stop My Heart from Loving
    You
Kapp, Richard
  Battle Lines
  Can I Let Her Go
Kaz, Eric
  That's What Love Is All About
Keane, Tom
  The Secret of My Success
  Will You Still Love Me
Keifer, Tom
  Nobody's Fool
Kelly, Eban
  You and Me Tonight
Kelly, Rick
  I Do You
Kelly, Tom
  Alone
  In My Dreams
  So Emotional
Kendricks, Kevin
  Back and Forth
Kennedy, Mary Ann
  I'll Still Be Loving You
Kennerly, Paul
  Cry Myself to Sleep
Kimball, Jennifer
  I Will Be There
King, Jay
  Why You Treat Me So Bad
King, Mark
  Lessons in Love
  Running in the Family
Kipner, Steve
  If She Would Have Been Faithful
Klender, R.
  Dear Mr. Jesus

136

McKinney, Jimmy
I Don't Want to Lose Your Love
McLaughlin, Pat
Lynda
McLeod, Bill
The Honey Thief
McMann, Gerard
Cry Little Sister (Theme from *The Lost Boys*)
McNally, Terrence
The Homecoming Queen's Got a Gun
I Like 'Em Big and Stupid
McVie, Christine
Little Lies
Meier, Dieter
Oh Yeah
Mellencamp, John
Paper in Fire
Mellencamp, John Cougar
Cherry Bomb
Merchant, Natalie
Hey, Jack Kerouac
Verdi Cries
Merrill, Gary
I Wanna Dance with Somebody (Who Loves Me)
Merrill, George
Simply Meant to Be
Michael, Brett
I Won't Forget You
Michael, George
Faith
I Want Your Sex
Michael, M.
Carrie
Michaels, Brett
Talk Dirty to Me
Mills, Kevin
I Go Crazy
Mills, Mike
Even a Dog Can Shake Hands
It's the End of the World as We Know It (and I Feel Fine)
The One I Love
Romance
Minnifield, E.
Hold Me

Mitchell, James
I Go Crazy
Mizell, Jason
Christmas in Hollis
Mohr, Joseph
Silent Night
Moir, Monte
The Pleasure Principle
Moman, Chips
Partners After All
Monk, Debbie
Ohio Afternoon
Montgomery, Bob
Back in Baby's Arms
Moore
Learning to Fly
Moore, B.
One for the Money
Moore, K.
You and Me Tonight
Morales, Mark
Protect Yourself/My Nuts
More, Julian
House in Algiers
Morgan, Dennis
I Knew You Were Waiting (for Me)
Moroder, Giorgio
Meet Me Half Way
Winner Takes All
Morris, Gary
Leave Me Lonely
Morrison, Bob
Whiskey, If You Were a Woman
Mould, Bob
No Reservations
Mugrage, Michael
So Different Now
Murphy, Mic
Don't Disturb This Groove
Murrah, Roger
It Takes a Little Rain
This Crazy Love
Myers, Frank
You're Never Too Old for Young Love

Ware, Leon
  You Make Me Want to Love Again
Warren, Diana
  Nothing's Gonna Stop Us Now
Warren, Diane
  Deeper Love
  Who Will You Run To
Waterman, Pete
  I Heard a Rumour
Waters, Roger
  Radio Waves
Waterson, Jack
  Sorry Naomi
Watley, Jody
  Don't You Want Me
  Looking for a New Love
  Still a Thrill
Watson, B.
  Rock Steady
Webber, Andrew Lloyd
  All I Ask of You
  Light at the End of the Tunnel
  The Music of the Night
  Only You
  Starlight Express
Weil, Cynthia
  Love Lives On
Weiss, Elliot
  Dungeons and Dragons
  Mama Don't Cry
  Our Favorite Restaurant
Welch, Kevin
  Fewer Threads than These
West, Rick
  Trouble in the Fields
Westerberg, Paul
  Can't Hardly Wait
White, Andy
  Reality Row
White, Mark
  When Smokey Sings
Whitehead, John
  I Don't Want to Lose Your Love
Whitlock, Tom
  Criminal (Theme from *Fatal Beauty*)
  Meet Me Half Way

Winner Takes All
Widelitz, Stacey
  She's Like the Wind
Williams, Hank, Jr.
  Born to Boogie
Williams, M.
  One for the Money
Willis, Allee
  Be There
  Live My Life
  What Have I Done to Deserve This
Wilson, Brian
  Let's Go to Heaven in My Car
Wilson, Nancy
  There's the Girl
Wimbley, Damon
  Protect Yourself/My Nuts
Winbush, Angela
  Angel
  Show Me the Way
  Smooth Sailin' Tonight
Winwood, Steve
  Back in the High Life Again
  The Finer Things
  Valerie
Wolf, Peter
  Come As You Are
Wonder, Stevie
  Skeletons
Woodward, Keren
  I Heard a Rumour
Workman, Lyle
  I Don't Mind at All
Wright, M.
  I Prefer the Moonlight
Wright, Robert
  The Broken Pianolita
Yoakam, Dwight
  Readin,' Rightin,' Route 23
Young, George
  Good Times
Young, Neil
  We've Never Danced
Zanes, Dan
  Long Slide (for an Out)
  News from Nowhere
Zevon, Warren
  Detox Mansion

Important Performances Index

Songs are listed under the works in which they were introduced or given significant renditions. The index is organized into major sections by performance medium: Album, Movie, Musical, Revue, Television Show, Vocalist.

Album

ABC in Alphabet City
  When Smokey Sings
Actually
  It's a Sin
  What Have I Done to Deserve
  This
All by Myself
  Show Me the Way
All Fool's Day
  Just Like Fire Would
All in the Name of Love
  Always
All Systems Go
  Dinner with Gershwin
Always and Forever
  Forever and Ever, Amen
  I Won't Need You Anymore
  (Always and Forever)
Americana
  A Long Line of Love
Another Step
  You Keep Me Hanging On
Another Woman's Man
  Another Woman's Man

Aretha
  I Knew You Were Waiting (for
  Me)
  Jimmy Lee
At My Window
  For the Sake of the Song
At Yankee Stadium
  I Want You Bad
August
  Bad Influence
  Tearing Us Apart
Baby Tonight
  Don't Go
Babylon and On
  Hourglass
Back for the Attack
  Dream Warriors
Back in the High Life
  The Finer Things
Back in the High Life Again
  Back in the High Life Again
Back to Basics
  A New England
Back to the Beach
  Surfin' Bird

The Living Daylights
 The Living Daylights
Living in a Box
 Living in a Box
London 0 Hull 4
 Happy Hour
London O Hull 4
 Sitting on a Fence
Lone Star State of Mind
 Beacon Street
 Cold Hearts/Closed Minds
 Ford Econoline
 From a Distance
 Lone Star State of Mind
 There's a Light beyond These
  Woods (Mary Margaret)
 Trouble in the Fields
The Lonesome Jubilee
 Cherry Bomb
 Paper in Fire
Long Live the New Flesh
 I Go Crazy
Long Time Coming
 Love You Down
Look What the Cat Dragged In
 I Won't Forget You
 Talk Dirty to Me
Lose Your Cool
 Good Times
The Lost Boys
 Cry Little Sister (Theme from *The
  Lost Boys*)
 Good Times
Lost in the Fifties Tonight
 How Do I Turn You On
Love an Adventure
 Funkytown
Love Me Like You Used To
 Love Me Like You Used To
Love Will Find Its Way to You
 Mornin' Ride
Lyle Lovett
 God Will
Mad, Bad, and Dangerous to Know
 Brand New Lover
Made in Heaven
 Romance
 We've Never Danced

Magic
 I Do You
Meet Danny Wilson
 Mary's Prayer
Michael Feinstein Sings Irving Berlin
 Looking at You (across the
  Breakfast Table)
Midnight to Midnight
 Heartbreak Beat
A Momentary Lapse of Reason
 Learning to Fly
Moonlighting
 Moonlighting (Theme)
More Love Songs
 The Back Nine
 Hard Day on the Planet
 I Eat Out
Mosaic
 Hypnotize Me
 Let's Go
Music and Songs from Starlight
 Express
 Light at the End of the Tunnel
Music and Songs from "Starlight
 Express"
 Only You
 Starlight Express
Never Enough
 Downtown Train
 Sue Lee
Never Let Me Down
 Day in--Day Out
Night Songs
 Nobody's Fool
No Protection
 It's Not Over ('Til It's Over)
Nothing Like the Sun
 They Dance Alone
 We'll Be Together
Ocean Front Property
 All My Ex's Live in Texas
 Am I Blue
 Ocean Front Property
The O'Kanes
 Can't Stop My Heart from Loving
  You

152

On the Front Line
  I Will Be There
  Three Time Loser
  You Still Move Me
One for the Money
  One for the Money
One Heartbeat
  Just to See Her
  One Heartbeat
One Way Home
  Satellite
One World
  What Are We Making Weapons
    For
Out of the Blue
  Only in My Dreams
  Shake Your Love
Over the Top
  Meet Me Half Way
  Winner Takes All
Partners
  Partners After All
Permanent Vacation
  Dude (Looks Like a Lady)
The Phantom of the Opera
  All I Ask of You
  The Music of the Night
A Place Called Love
  I'll Be Your Baby Tonight
Plain Brown Wrapper
  Leave Me Lonely
Planes, Trains, and Automobiles
  Back in Baby's Arms
Platoon
  White Rabbit
Pleased to Meet Me
  Can't Hardly Wait
Police Academy 4
  Let's Go to Heaven in My Car
Primitive Cool
  Let's Work
The Princess Bride
  Storybook Love
Private Revolution
  Ship of Fools (Save Me from
    Tomorrow)
Radio K.A.O.S.
  Radio Waves

Raised on Radio
  I'll Be Alright without You
Rave On
  Reality Row
Ready or Not
  Midnight Blue
Reba McEntire's Greatest Hits
  One Promise Too Late
Recently
  Biko
Reservations for Two
  Love Power
The Return of Bruno
  Under the Boardwalk
Revenge of the Nerds
  Back to Paradise
Richard Marx
  Don't Mean Nothin
  Should've Known Better
Right Hand Man
  Right Hand Man
  Shine, Shine, Shine
  You're Never Too Old for Young
    Love
Robbie Nevil
  Dominoes
  Wot's It to Ya
Robbie Robertson
  Fallen Angel
  Somewhere Down the Crazy River
  Sweet Fire of Love
Rockin' with the Rhythm
  Cry Myself to Sleep
Rogers, Kenny
  I Prefer the Moonlight
Romeo's Escape
  Fourth of July
Running in the Family
  Lessons in Love
  Running in the Family
The Secret of My Success
  The Secret of My Success
See How We Are
  Fourth of July
Sentimental Hygiene
  Detox Mansion
  Even a Dog Can Shake Hands

Time
  Something in Your Eyes
Timothy B.
  Boys Night Out
Together Again
  I Wonder Who She's Seeing Now
Too Many Times
  I Can't Win for Losin' You
  I Need a Good Woman Bad
  That Was a Close One
The Touch
  –You've Got" The Touch
Touch and Go
  Love Is a House
Touch Me
  Touch Me (I Want Your Body)
Touch the World
  System of Survival
T'Pau
  Heart and Soul
Trapped in the Body of a White Girl
  The Homecoming Queen's Got a
    Gun
  I Like 'Em Big and Stupid
Trio
  Telling Me Lies
  To Know Him Is to Love Him
True Blue
  La Isla Bonita
True Colors
  What's Going On
Trust Your Heart
  Jerusalem
Tunnel of Love
  Brilliant Disguise
  One Step Up
  Spare Parts
  Tunnel of Love
  Valentine's Day
  Walk Like a Man
Two Fisted Tales
  I Want You Bad
2 Live Crew Is What We Are
  We Want Some Pussy
2400 Fulton Street
  White Rabbit
Unlimited
  I Want to Be Your Man

Vega, Suzanne
  Gypsy
A Very Special Christmas
  Christmas (Baby Please Come
    Home)
  Christmas in Hollis
  Do You Hear What I Hear
  Have Yourself a Merry Little
    Christmas
  The Little Drummer Boy
  Santa Baby
  Silent Night
  Winter Wonderland
Vesta
  You Make Me Want to Love Again
Vital Idol
  Mony Mony
Warehouse
  No Reservations
Watley, Jody
  Looking for a New Love
The Way It Is
  Every Little Kiss
What If We Fall in Love
  Another World
Wheels
  I'll Still Be Loving You
  Why Does It Have to Be (Wrong
    or Right)
Where the Fast Lane Ends
  It Takes a Little Rain
  This Crazy Love
Whiplash Smile
  Sweet Sixteen
Whitesnake
  Here I Go Again
  In This Love
  Still of the Night
Whitney
  Didn't We Almost Have It All
  I Know Him So Well
  I Wanna Dance with Somebody
    (Who Loves Me)
  So Emotional
Who Found Who
  Who Found Who
The Whole Story
  Cloudbusting

Who's That Girl
  Causing a Commotion
  Who's That Girl
Wild Eyed Dream
  Somebody Lied
Wings
  The Moon Is Still Over Her
   Shoulder
Wishes
  Goodbye Saving Grace
Word Up
  Back and Forth
  Candy
Yo Yo
  I Don't Mind at All
You Again
  You Again
The Zagora
  Slow Down

Movie

Baby Boom
  Everchanging Times
Back to the Beach
  Surfin' Bird
Beverly Hills Cop II
  Be There
  Cross My Broken Heart
  I Want Your Sex
  Shakedown
Blind Date
  Simply Meant to Be
Burglar
  Time Out for the Burglar
Chariots of Fire
  Jerusalem
Dirty Dancing
  She's Like the Wind
  You Don't Own Me

Disorderlies
  I Heard a Rumour
  Wipe Out
Down by Law
  Downtown Train
Dragnet
  City of Crime
  Dragnet
  Just the Facts
Fatal Beauty
  Criminal (Theme from *Fatal Beauty*)
Fenton, George and Jonas Gwangwa
  Cry Freedom
Ferris Beuller's Day Off
  Oh Yeah
The Golden Child
  Deeper Love
Harry and the Hendersons
  Love Lives On
Hearts of Fire
  Had a Dream About You, Baby
  Night After Night
Hiding Out
  Catch Me (I'm Falling)
  Live My Life
  So Different Now
Inner Space
  Hypnotize Me
Ishtar
  Little Darlin'
La Bamba
  La Bamba
Less than Zero
  Hazy Shade of Winter
  In-A-Gadda-Da-Vida
Lethal Weapon
  Lethal Weapon
Light of Day
  Light of Day
The Living Daylights
  The Living Daylights
The Lost Boys
  Cry Little Sister (Theme from *The Lost Boys*)
  Good Times

Musical

Three Postcards
  She Was K.C. at Seven

Operetta
Magdelena
  The Broken Pianolita

Play
Mama Drama
  I Love My Mom

Revue
The No-Frills Revue
  Privacy

Television Show
Another World
  Another World
Ask Dr. Ruth
  Protect Yourself/My Nuts
Moonlighting
  Moonlighting (Theme)
Private Eye
  Blue Hotel
'S Wonderful
  Lonely Boy
We the People 200
  Let Freedom Ring
A Week with Raquel/7-Day Wake Up
  and Shape Up
  This Girl's Back in Town

Vocalist
ABC
  When Smokey Sings
Adams, Bryan
  Hearts on Fire
  Heat of the Night
Aerosmith
  Dude (Looks Like a Lady)

Aiello, Josie, and Peter Hewlett
  Only You
Alabama
  You've Got   The Touch
Allen, Deborah
  Telepathy
Allison, Mose
  Ever Since the World Ended
  I Looked in the Mirror
  Putting Up with Me
Alpert, Herb
  Diamonds
Alvin, Dave
  Fourth of July
Art of Noise
  Dragnet
Atlantic Starr
  Always
Aykroyd, Dan
  City of Crime
Baez, Joan
  Biko
Bakker, Tammy Faye
  The Ballad of Jim and Tammy
Bananarama
  I Heard a Rumour
Bangles
  Hazy Shade of Winter
The Barbusters
  Light of Day
Barton, Steve
  All I Ask of You
Beastie Boys
  (You Gotta) Fight for Your Right
  (to Party)
Bee Gees
  You Win Again
Bellamy Brothers
  Crazy from the Heart
  Kids of the Baby Boom
Belle, Regina
  Show Me the Way
Benitez, Jellybean
  Who Found Who
Blow Monkeys
  You Don't Own Me
Bogardus, Stephen
  I've Noticed a Change

Important Performances Index — Vocalist

Bolton, Michael
  That's What Love Is All About
Bon Jovi
  Livin' on a Prayer
  Wanted Dead or Alive
Boston
  Can'tcha Say (You Believe in Me)
  We're Ready
Bourgeois Tagg
  I Don't Mind at All
Bowie, David
  Day in--Day Out
Boy George
  Live My Life
Bragg, Billy
  A New England
Breakfast Club
  Expressway to Your Heart
  Right on Track
Brightman, Sarah
  All I Ask of You
Brown, Georgia
  House in Algiers
Brown, Julie
  The Homecoming Queen's Got a
    Gun
  I Like 'Em Big and Stupid
Brown, T. Graham
  Don't Go to Strangers
Bush, Kate
  Cloudbusting
Butcher, Jon
  Goodbye Saving Grace
California Raisins
  I Heard It through the Grapevine
Callaway, Liz
  I've Noticed a Change
Cameo
  Back and Forth
  Candy
Cariou, Len
  Can I Let Her Go
Carlisle, Belinda
  Heaven Is a Place on Earth
Carnelia, Craig
  She Was K.C. at Seven
Carpenter, Mary Chapin
  Downtown Train

Carpenter, Richard and Dusty
    Springfield
  Something in Your Eyes
Cars
  You Are the Girl
Cash, Rosanne
  The Way We Make a Broken Heart
Casson-Jellison, Claudine
  Mama Don't Cry
Cavaliere, Felix
  So Different Now
Cher
  I Found Someone
Chicago
  If She Would Have Been Faithful
  Will You Still Love Me
Cinderella
  Nobody's Fool
Clapton, Eric
  Bad Influence
  Tearing Us Apart
Club Nouveau
  Lean on Me
  Why You Treat Me So Bad
Cocker, Joe
  Love Lives On
Cole, Natalie
  Jump Start
  Pink Cadillac
Collins, Judy
  Jerusalem
Conley, Earl Thomas
  I Can't Win for Losin' You
  I Need a Good Woman Bad
  That Was a Close One
Crawford, Michael
  The Music of the Night
Cray, Robert
  Right Next Door (Because of Me)
  Smoking Gun.
Crivello, Anthony
  Drink with Me to Days Gone By
Crowded House
  Don't Dream It's Over
  Something So Strong
  World Where You Live
The Cult
  Born to Be Wild

159

Jennings, Waylon
  Rose in Paradise
Jets
  Cross My Broken Heart
  I Do You
  You Got It All
Joan Jett and the Blackhearts
  You Got Me Floating
John, Elton
  Candle in the Wind
Johnson, Michael
  The Moon Is Still Over Her
    Shoulder
Jones, David Lynn
  Bonnie Jean (Little Sister)
  Living in the Promiseland
Jones, Glenn
  We've Only Just Begun (The
    Romance Is Not Over)
Journey
  I'll Be Alright without You
Judds
  Cry Myself to Sleep
  I Know Where I'm Going
  Maybe Your Baby's Got the Blues
K., Tonio
  I'm Supposed to Have Sex with
    You
Kenyon, Joe
  Hymne
Klymaxx
  I'd Still Say Yes
Kool and the Gang
  Stone Love
Kool Moe Dee
  Go See the Doctor
Kydd, John
  Up the Ladder to the Roof
La Belle, Patti
  Just the Facts
Lauper, Cyndi
  What's Going On
Lavin, Christine
  Another Woman's Man
Level 42
  Lessons in Love
  Running in the Family

Levert
  Casanova
  My Forever Love
Lewis, Huey and the News
  Doing It All for My Baby
  I Know What I Like
Lillo
  I'm in Love
Lisa Lisa and Cult Jam
  Head to Toe
  Lost in Emotion
Little Steven
  Bitter Fruit
  Trail of Broken Treaties
Living in a Box
  Living in a Box
Lizardo, Maribel
  Don't Come Inside My Head
LL Cool J
  I Need Love
Loggins, Kenny
  Meet Me Half Way
The Long Ryders
  I Want You Bad
Loose Ends
  Slow Down
Los Lobos
  The Hardest Time
  La Bamba
  One Time One Night
  River of Fools
  Set Me Free (Rosa Lee)
Lovett, Lyle
  God Will
Lynch, Ray
  Celestial Soda Pop
MacColl, Kirsty
  A New England
Madonna
  Causing a Commotion
  La Isla Bonita
  Santa Baby
  Who's That Girl
Manilow, Barry
  Let Freedom Ring
Marx, Richard
  Don't Mean Nothin
  Should've Known Better

Pomeranz, David and Sasha Malinin
Far Away Lands
PowerSource
Dear Mr. Jesus
Pretenders
Have Yourself a Merry Little
Christmas
Pretty Poison
Catch Me (I'm Falling)
Prince
Housequake
I Could Never Take the Place of
Your Man
It's Gonna Be a Beautiful Night
Sign 'o' the Times
U Got the Look
Principato, Tom
My Baby Worships Me
Prine, John
Let's Talk Dirty in Hawaiian
Out of Love
Pseudo Echo
Funkytown
Psychedelic Furs
Heartbreak Beat
Raitt, John
The Broken Pianolita
Raven, Eddy
Right Hand Man
Shine, Shine, Shine
You're Never Too Old for Young
Love
Ready for the World
Love You Down
The Red Army Chorus
Love Lights the World
(Rendezvous)
R.E.M.
It's the End of the World as We
Know It (and I Feel Fine)
The One I Love
Romance
REO Speedwagon
In My Dreams
Reo Speedwagon
That Ain't Love
Replacements
Can't Hardly Wait

Restless Heart
I'll Still Be Loving You
Why Does It Have to Be (Wrong
or Right)
Richie, Lionel
Ballerina Girl
Robertson, Robbie
Fallen Angel
Somewhere Down the
Crazy River
Sweet Fire of Love
Robinson, Smokey
Just to See Her
One Heartbeat
Roches
I Love My Mom
Rodman, Judy
I'll Be Your Baby Tonight
Roger
I Want to Be Your Man
Rogers, Kenny
Twenty Years Ago
Rooney, Jan
Love Is Being Loved
Ruffelle, Frances
On My Own
Run DMC
Christmas in Hollis
Rush, Jennifer and Elton John
Flames of Paradise
Saints
Just Like Fire Would
Schmidt, Timothy B.
Boys Night Out
Schneider, John
Love, You Ain't Seen the Last of
Me
Schuyler, Knobloch & Overstreet
American Me
Baby's Got a New Baby
Seals, Dan
I Will Be There
Three Time Loser
You Still Move Me
Seger, Bob
The Little Drummer Boy
Shakedown

Awards Index

A list of songs nominated for Academy Awards by the Academy of Motion Picture Arts and Sciences and Grammy Awards from the National Academy of Recording Arts and Sciences. Asterisks indicate the winners.

1987

Academy Award
  Cry Freedom
  Nothing's Gonna Stop Us Now
  Shakedown
  Storybook Love
  (I've Had) The Time of My Life*

Country Music Association Award
  Forever and Ever, Amen

Grammy Award
  All My Ex's Live in Texas
  Back in the High Life Again
  Casanova
  Didn't We Almost Have It All
  80's Ladies
  Forever and Ever, Amen*

Graceland*
I Still Haven't Found What I'm
  Looking For
I'll Still Be Loving You
Just to See Her
La Bamba
Lean on Me
Luka
Moonlighting (Theme)
Nothing's Gonna Stop Us Now
Skeletons
Somewhere Out There*
Somewhere Out There
Telling Me Lies
(I've Had) The Time of My Life
U Got the Look

List of Publishers

A directory of publishers of the songs included in *Popular Music,* 1987. Publishers that are members of the American Society of Composers, Authors, and Publishers or whose catalogs are available under ASCAP license are indicated by the designation (ASCAP). Publishers that have granted performing rights to Broadcast Music, Inc., are designated by the notation (BMI). Publishers whose catalogs are represented by SESAC, Inc., are indicated by the designation (SESAC).

The addresses were gleaned from a variety of sources, including ASCAP, BMI, SESAC, *Billboard* magazine, and the National Music Publishers' Association. As in any volatile industry, many of the addresses may become outdated quickly. In the interim between the book's completion and its subsequent publication, some publishers may have been consolidated into others or changed hands. This is a fact of life long endured by the music business and its constituents. The data collected here, and throughout the book, are as accurate as such circumstances allow.

A

Acara (ASCAP)
see WB Music Corp.

Ackee Music Inc. (ASCAP)
see Island Music

Acuff Rose Opryland (BMI)
P.O. Box 121900
Nashville, Tennessee 37212

Adams Communications, Inc. (BMI)
see Almo Music Corp.

Aerodynamics
Address unknown

AGF Music Ltd. (ASCAP)
1500 Broadway, Suite 2805
New York, New York 10036

Air Bear (BMI)
c/o Warner-Tamerlane
9000 Sunset Blvd.
Los Angeles, California 90069

Alabama Band Music Co. (ASCAP)
803 18th Avenue S.
Nashville, Tennessee 37203

171

All Seeing Eye Music (ASCAP)
1422 West Peachtree Street, N.W.
Suite 816
Atlanta, Georgia 30309

Almo Music Corp. (ASCAP)
1416 N. La Brea Avenue
Hollywood, California 90028

AMR (ASCAP)
808 19th Avenue, S.
Nashville, Tennessee 37203

Angel Notes (ASCAP)
see WB Music Corp.

Applied Action (ASCAP)
Address unknown

Appogiatura Music Inc. (BMI)
c/o Franklin, Weinrib, Rudell &
Vasallo
950 Third Avenue
New York, New York 10022

April Music, Inc. (ASCAP)
49 E. 52nd Street
New York, New York 10022

Arista Music, Inc.
8370 Wilshire Blvd.
Beverly Hills, California 90211

Atlantic Music Corp. (BMI)
6124 Selma Avenue
Hollywood, California 90028

Attadoo (BMI)
c/o Bobby Emmons
Johnson Chapel Road
Brentwood, Tennessee 37027

Attractive (BMI)
Address unknown

ATV Music Corp. (BMI)
c/o ATV Group
6255 Sunset Blvd.
Hollywood, California 90028

Audre Mae Music (BMI)
34 Dogwood Drive
Smithtown, New York 11787

Avant Garde Music Publishing, Inc.
(ASCAP)
Att: Clarence Avant
9229 Sunset Blvd., No. 331
Los Angeles, California 90069

B

Bait and Beer (ASCAP)
c/o Terrell Tye
PO 120657
Nashville, Tennessee 37212

Denise Barry Music (ASCAP)
c/o Peter T. Paterno, Esq.
Manatt, Phelps, Rothenberg & Tunney
11355 W. Olympic Blvd.
Los Angeles, California 90064

Beach Bum (BMI)
c/o Mason & Sloane
1299 Ocean Avenue
Santa Monica, California 90401

Beachead (ASCAP)
Address unknown

Beckaroo (BMI)
PO 150272
Nashville, Tennessee 37215

Beginner Music (ASCAP)
c/o Kevin Lamb & Associates
P.O. Box 2921
Florence, Alabama 35630

Bellamy Brothers Music (ASCAP)
P.O. Box 294
Route 2
Dade City, Florida 33525

Bellboy Music (BMI)
Att: Earl Shelton
309 S. Broad Street
Philadelphia, Pennsylvania 19107

Better Days Music (BMI)
  Moultrie Accountancy Corp.
  Att: Fred S. Moultrie, C.P.A.
  P.O. Box 5270
  Beverly Hills, California 90210

Bibo Music Publishers (ASCAP)
  see Welk Music Group

Big Ears Music Inc. (ASCAP)
  c/o Sy Miller
  565 Fifth Avenue, Suite 1001
  New York, New York 10017

Big Thrilling Music (ASCAP)
  see Of the Fire Music

Big Tooth Music Corp. (ASCAP)
  see Rare Blue Music, Inc.

Bilt (BMI)
  see Bug Music

Bittersuite Co.
  Address unknown

Bittersuite Co.
  Address unknown

Black Bull Music (ASCAP)
  Att: Stevland Morris
  4616 Magnolia Blvd.
  Burbank, California 91505

Black Lion (ASCAP)
  6525 Sunset Blvd., 2nd Fl.
  Hollywood, California 90028

Black Sheep Music Inc. (BMI)
  1009 17th Avenue, S.
  Nashville, Tennessee 37212

Blackwood Music Inc. (BMI)
  1350 Avenue of the Americas
  23rd Fl.
  New York, New York 10019

Bleu Disque Music (ASCAP)
  c/o Warner Brothers Music
  9000 Sunset Blvd., Penthouse
  Los Angeles, California 90069

Blue Horn Toad (BMI)
  see Bug Music

Blue Lake Music (BMI)
  c/o Terrace Music
  818 18th Avenue, S.
  Nashville, Tennessee 37203

Blue Quill Music (ASCAP)
  see Cherry Lane Music Co., Inc.

Blue Sky Rider Songs (BMI)
  c/o Prager and Fenton
  6363 Sunset Blvd., Suite 706
  Los Angeles, California 90028

Blue Water (BMI)
  Address unknown

BMG (ASCAP)
  Address unknown

Bob-a-Lew Songs (ASCAP)
  P.O. Box 8031
  Universal City, California 91608

Bocephus Music Inc. (BMI)
  see Singletree Music Co., Inc.

Bon Jovi Publishing (ASCAP)
  c/o Siegel & Feldstein
  509 Madison Avenue
  New York, New York 10022

Boneidol Music (ASCAP)
  c/o Aucoin Management Inc.
  645 Madison Avenue
  New York, New York 10022

Alain Boublil Music Inc. (ASCAP)
  1776 Broadway
  New York, New York 10019

Bourgeoise Zee (ASCAP)
  Address unknown

173

List of Publishers

Boy Meets Girl (BMI)
see Irving Music Inc.

Brenee (BMI)
c/o Miller-Ward & Co.
9060 Santa Monica Blvd.
Los Angeles, California 90060

Brockman Enterprises Inc. (ASCAP)
Leibren Music Division
c/o Jess S. Morgan & Co., Inc.
6420 Wilshire Blvd., 19th Fl.
Los Angeles, California 90048

Brooklyn Dust (ASCAP)
see Def Jam

Broozertoones, Inc. (ASCAP)
c/o Segel, Goldman & Macnow Inc.
9348 Santa Monica Blvd.
Beverly Hills, California 90210

Bruised Oranges (ASCAP)
c/o Sy Miller
565 Fifth Avenue, Suite 1001
New York, New York 10017

Bug Music (BMI)
Bug Music Group
6777 Hollywood Blvd., 9th Fl.
Hollywood, California 90028

Burger Bits (ASCAP)
Address unknown

Bush Burnin' Music (ASCAP)
1020 Grand Concourse, Suite 17W
Bronx, New York 10451

But For (ASCAP)
Address unknown

Larry Butler Music Co. (ASCAP)
P.O. Box 121318
Nashville, Tennessee 37212

Butler's Bandits (ASCAP)
SBK Songs
810 Seventh Avenue
New York, New York 10019

Buy Rum (ASCAP)
see WB Music Corp.

C

Cak Songs (ASCAP)
c/o Entertainment Music Co.
1700 Broadway, 41st Fl.
New York, New York 10019

Calhoun Street (BMI)
see Bug Music

California Phase Music (ASCAP)
c/o Fitzgerald Hartley Co.
7250 Beverly Blvd., Suite 200
Los Angeles, California 90036

Calloco
Address unknown

Calypso Toonz (BMI)
see Irving Music Inc.

Camp Songs Music (BMI)
c/o Gottlieb, Schiff, Ticktin,
Sternklar & Singer
Att: Mark D. Sendroff
555 Fifth Avenue
New York, New York 10017

Camper Von Beethoven Music
Address unknown

Carbert Music Inc. (BMI)
1619 Broadway, Rm. 609
New York, New York 10019

Careers Music Inc. (ASCAP)
see Arista Music, Inc.

Buzz Cason Publications Inc. (ASCAP)
2804 Azalea Place
Nashville, Tennessee 37204

Cavesson Music Enterprises Co. (ASCAP)
Joiner Music Division
Lariat Music Co. Division
815 18th Avenue, S.
Nashville, Tennessee 37203

CBS-Robbins (ASCAP)
Address unknown

CBS Unart Catalog Inc. (BMI)
49 E. 52nd Street
New York, New York 10022

CC (ASCAP)
Address unknown

Ceros (BMI)
see Bug Music

C'est Music (ASCAP)
see Quackenbush Music, Ltd.

Chappell & Co., Inc. (ASCAP)
810 Seventh Avenue
New York, New York 10019

Cherry Lane Music Co., Inc. (ASCAP)
110 Midland Avenue
Port Chester, New York 10573

Cherry Mountain (ASCAP)
see Cherry Lane Music Co., Inc.

ChiBoy (ASCAP)
Address unknown

Chips Moman (BMI)
PO 3145
Memphis, Tennessee 38103

Christian Burial (ASCAP)
Address unknown

Chriswald Music (ASCAP)
6255 Sunset Blvd., Suite 1911
Hollywood, California 90028

Chrysalis Music Corp. (ASCAP)
Chrysalis Music Group
645 Madison Avenue
New York, New York 10022

Chubu (BMI)
c/o Iglow & Bachrach
1515 N. Crescent Heights Blvd.
Los Angeles, California 90046

Coal Dust West (BMI)
c/o William A. Coben
2029 Century Park E.
Los Angeles, California 90067

Colgems-EMI Music Inc. (ASCAP)
see Screen Gems-EMI Music Inc.

Tom Collins Music Corp. (BMI)
P.O. Box 121407
Nashville, Tennessee 37212

Colloco (ASCAP)
Address unknown

Controversy Music (ASCAP)
c/o Manatt, Phelps, Rothenberg
Att: Lee Phillips
11355 W. Olympic Blvd.
Los Angeles, California 90064

Coolwell Music (ASCAP)
c/o Granite Music Corp.
6124 Selma Avenue
Los Angeles, California 90028

Copyright Control (ASCAP)
see Bug Music

Cotillion Music Inc. (BMI)
75 Rockefeller Plaza, 2nd Fl.
New York, New York 10019

Robert Cray (BMI)
1315 Third Avenue W.
Seattle, Washington 98119

Creative Bloc (ASCAP)
Address unknown

Criterion Music Corp. (ASCAP)
6124 Selma Avenue
Hollywood, California 90028

Cross Keys Publishing Co., Inc. (ASCAP)
see Tree Publishing Co., Inc.

List of Publishers

Crosstown (ASCAP)
c/o J. Hilliard
1427 N. Laurel Avenue
Hollywood, California 90046

Crush Club (BMI)
c/o David A. Braun
2029 Century Park E.
Suite 1900
Los Angeles, California 90067

D

Danny Tunes (BMI)
c/o Iglow & Bachrach
1515 N. Crescent Heights Blvd.
Los Angeles, California 90046

Davince Music (ASCAP)
c/o Bug Music Group
6777 Hollywood Blvd., 9th Fl.
Hollywood, California 90028

Deborah Anne (ASCAP)
Address unknown

Def Jam (ASCAP)
5 University Place
New York, New York 10003

Delightful Music Ltd. (BMI)
c/o Mr. Ted Eddy
200 W. 57th Street
New York, New York 10019

Deshufflin' Inc.
c/o Michael Tannen, Esq.
36 E. 61st Street
New York, New York 10021

Desmobile Music Co. (ASCAP)
Att: Desmond Child
12 W. 72nd Street
New York, New York 10023

Dillard (BMI)
c/o Gopam Enterprises
11 Riverside Drive
New York, New York 10023

Donald Jay (ASCAP)
Address unknown

Downstairs Music, Inc. (BMI)
c/o Earl Shelton
309 S. Broad Street
Philadelphia, Pennsylvania 19107

Dramatis Music Corp. (BMI)
see EMP Co.

Dub Notes (ASCAP)
c/o Levine & Thall, PC
485 Madison Avenue
New York, New York 10022

E

E/A (BMI)
c/o Warner-Tamerlane
9000 Sunset Blvd.
Los Angeles, California 90069

Earthly Delights (BMI)
c/o Gary Scruggs
774 Elysian Fields Road
Nashville, Tennessee 37204

Edge of Fluke (ASCAP)
Address unknown

Emboe (ASCAP)
see April Music, Inc.

EMP Co. (BMI)
The Entertainment Co.
40 W. 57th Street
New York, New York 10019

End of the Trail (ASCAP)
see Bug Music

Ensign Music Corp. (BMI)
c/o Sidney Herman
1 Gulf & Western Plaza
New York, New York 10023

Enthralled (ASCAP)
Address unknown

Eve (ASCAP)
see Chappell & Co., Inc.

Evie Music Inc. (ASCAP)
see Chappell & Co., Inc.

F

Face the Music (BMI)
c/o Warner Brothers Music
44 Music Square, W.
Nashville, Tennessee 37203

Famous Music Corp. (ASCAP)
Gulf & Western Industries, Inc.
1 Gulf & Western Plaza
New York, New York 10023

Fat Boys (ASCAP)
Address unknown

Fate Music (ASCAP)
1046 Carol Drive
Los Angeles, California 90069

Fave Rave (BMI)
Address unknown

Ferncliff (BMI)
c/o Harry J. Coombs
110112 Lantoga Road
Wayne, Pennsylvania 19087

Fiddleback Music Publishing Co., Inc.
(BMI)
1270 Avenue of the Americas
New York, New York 10020

Fire Mist (BMI)
2180 Stunt Road
Calabasas, California 90302

Five Storks (ASCAP)
see MCA Music

Fleetwood Mac Music Ltd. (BMI)
315 S. Beverly Drive, Suite 210
Beverly Hills, California 90212

Flip a Jig (ASCAP)
Address unknown

Flip 'n' Dog (BMI)
see MCA, Inc.

Flyte Tyme Tunes (ASCAP)
c/o Avant Garde Music Publishing
9229 Sunset Blvd., Suite 311
Los Angeles, California 90069

Forceful Music (BMI)
c/o Williston Music
PO 284
Brooklyn, New York 11203

Foreign Imported (BMI)
8921 S.W. Tenth Terrace
Miami, Florida 33174

Fountain Square Music Publishing Co.
Inc (ASCAP)
c/o Signature Sound Inc.
420 E. 72nd Street
New York, New York 10021

Frank Music Co. (ASCAP)
see MPL Communications Inc.

Franne Gee (ASCAP)
Address unknown

Future Furniture (ASCAP)
Att: Rick Nowels
7469 Melrose Avenue, No. 33
Los Angeles, California 90046

G

Gabeson (BMI)
c/o Meitus Copyright
2851 Laurana Road
Union, New Jersey 07083

Galleon Music, Inc. (ASCAP)
344 E. 49th Street, Suite 1A/B
New York, New York 10017

Ganga Publishing Co. (BMI)
see Screen Gems-EMI Music Inc.

Gear Publishing (ASCAP)
Division of Hideout Productions
567 Purdy
Birmingham, Michigan 48009

Geffen Music (ASCAP)
c/o Warner Bros. Music
9000 Sunset Blvd.
Los Angeles, California 90069

Genetic (ASCAP)
Address unknown

Genevieve Music (ASCAP)
c/o Bernard Gudvi & Co., Inc.
6420 Wilshire Blvd., No. 425
Los Angeles, California 90048

Gibb Brothers Music (BMI)
see Unichappell Music Inc.

GMPC (ASCAP)
see Giorgio Moroder Publishing Co.

Go Glow (ASCAP)
see Giorgio Moroder Publishing Co.

Bella Godiva Music (ASCAP)
see Chappell & Co., Inc.

Julie Gold Music (BMI)
242 W. Fourth Street
New York, New York 10014

Goldline Music Inc. (ASCAP)
see Silverline Music, Inc.

Goldpoint (ASCAP)
c/o Sound Stage Concepts
31 Girard Avenue
Bayshore, New York 11706

Michael H. Goldsen, Inc. (ASCAP)
6124 Selma Avenue
Hollywood, California 90028

Gomace Music, Inc. (BMI)
1000 N. Doheny Drive
Los Angeles, California 90069

Gone Gator Music (ASCAP)
c/o Bernard Gudvi & Co., Inc.
6420 Wilshire Blvd., Suite 425
Los Angeles, California 90048

Grand Pasha (BMI)
c/o Spencer D. Proffer
5615 Melrose Avenue
Los Angeles, California 90038

Grandma Annie Music (BMI)
c/o Sy Miller, Esq.
18 E. 48th Street, Suite 1202
New York, New York 10017

Granite Music Corp. (ASCAP)
6124 Selma Avenue
Hollywood, California 90028

Gratitude Sky Music, Inc. (ASCAP)
c/o Gelfand
2062 Union Street
San Francisco, California 94123

H

Rick Hall Music (ASCAP)
P.O. Box 2527
603 E. Avalon Avenue
Muscle Shoals, Alabama 35662

Hammer & Nails Music (ASCAP)
see Almo Music Corp.

Albert Hammond (ASCAP)
Address unknown

Bobby Hart (ASCAP)
see MCA Music

Hat Band Music (BMI)
The Sound Seventy Suite
210 25th Avenue, N.
Nashville, Tennessee 37203

He Gave Me (ASCAP)
see Almo Music Corp.

Heart Wheel (BMI)
PO 50603
Nashville, Tennessee 37205

Hidden Pun (BMI)
1841 Broadway
New York, New York 10023

Hideaway Hits (ASCAP)
c/o Scholz Research & Development
Corp.
1560 Trapelo Road
Waltham, Massachusetts 02154

High Varieties (ASCAP)
Address unknown

Hip Chic (BMI)
c/o Carter Tuner
9229 Sunset Blvd.
Los Angeles, California 90069

Hip-Trip Music Co. (BMI)
c/o Glen E. Davis
1635 N. Cahuenga Blvd., 6th Fl.
Hollywood, California 90028

Hit & Run Music (ASCAP)
1841 Broadway, Suite 411
New York, New York 10023

Hitwell (ASCAP)
Address unknown

Hobbler Music (ASCAP)
see WB Music Corp.

Hollysongs
Address unknown

Holmes Line of Music (ASCAP)
228 W. 71st Street
New York, New York 10023

Holsapple (BMI)
see Criterion Music Corp.

Hopi Sound Music (ASCAP)
c/o Chris De Walden
6255 Sunset Blvd., Suite 1911
Hollywood, California 90028

Hot Corner (ASCAP)
see WB Music Corp.

Nancy Hughes
see Famous Music Corp.

Hulex Music (BMI)
P.O. Box 819
Mill Valley, California 94942

Human Boy Music (ASCAP)
c/o Levine & Thall P.C.
485 Madison Avenue
New York, New York 10022

Husker Music (BMI)
P.O. Box 8646
Minneapolis, Minnesota 55408

I

Ice Nine Publishing Co., Inc. (ASCAP)
P.O. Box 1073
San Rafael, California 94915

Ides of March Music Division (ASCAP)
Wayfield Inc.
1136 Gateway Lane
Nashville, Tennessee 37220

If Dreams Had Wings (ASCAP)
c/o CMRRA
56 Wellesley Street, W.
Toronto, Ontario M5S 2S4
Canada

Illegal Songs, Inc. (BMI)
c/o Beverly Martin
633 N. La Brea Avenue
Hollywood, California 90036

Intersong, USA Inc.
c/o Chappell & Co., Inc.
810 Seventh Avenue
New York, New York 10019

List of Publishers

I.R.S. (BMI)
Address unknown

Irving Music Inc. (BMI)
1358 N. La Brea
Hollywood, California 90028

Is Hot Music, Ltd. (ASCAP)
34 Pheasant Run
Old Westbury, New York 11568

Chris Isaak Music Publishing (ASCAP)
Address unknown

Island Music (BMI)
c/o Mr. Lionel Conway
6525 Sunset Blvd.
Hollywood, California 90028

Island Visual Arts (ASCAP)
see Island Music

J

Jalma (ASCAP)
Address unknown

Dick James Music Inc. (BMI)
24 Music Square, E.
Nashville, Tennessee 37203

Jeddrah Music (ASCAP)
c/o Joel S. Morse
15910 Ventura Blvd., Suite 629
Encino, California 91436

Jemava (ASCAP)
Address unknown

Jobete Music Co., Inc. (ASCAP)
Att: Erlinda N. Barrios
6255 Sunset Blvd., Suite 1600
Hollywood, California 90028

Jodaway Music (ASCAP)
c/o Cole Classic Management
3030 W. Sixth Street, Suite 38
Los Angeles, California 90020

Johnny Yuma (BMI)
c/o Fitzgerald Hartley Co.
7250 Beverly Blvd.
Los Angeles, California 90036

David Lynn Jones (BMI)
Gelfand, Rennert & Feldman
7 Music Circle North
Nashville, Tennessee 37203

Jones Music Co.
c/o Dorothy Mae Rice Jones
1916 Portman Avenue
Cincinnati, Ohio 45237

Jonico Music Inc. (ASCAP)
Shubert, Silver & Rosen P.C.
316 E. 53rd Street
New York, New York 10022

JVA (ASCAP)
see April Music, Inc.

K

Kander & Ebb Inc. (BMI)
see Unichappell Music Inc.

Kieran Kane (ASCAP)
3607 Bellwood Drive
Nashville, Tennessee 37205

Kaz Music Co. (ASCAP)
P.O. Box 38
Woodstock, New York 12498

Kazoom (ASCAP)
see MCA Music

Rick Kelly (BMI)
4226 1/2 Gentry Avenue
Studio City, California 91604

Kilauea Music (BMI)
c/o On Music
4162 Lankershim Blvd.
Universal City, California 91602

Jay King, IV (BMI)
c/o Mitchell Silberberg
11377 W. Olympic Blvd.
Los Angeles, California 90064

Stephen A. Kipner Music (ASCAP)
Att: Stephen A. Kipner
19646 Valley View Drive
Topanga, California 90290

Klenco (ASCAP)
Address unknown

Klymaxx (ASCAP)
Address unknown

Knighty Knight (ASCAP)
see Arista Music, Inc.

Knockout Music Co. (ASCAP)
c/o Millennium Corp.
1619 Broadway, Suite 1209
New York, New York 10019

Know Music (ASCAP)
c/o VWC Management Inc.
13343 Bel Red Road, Suite 201
Bellevue, Washington 98005

Krell (BMI)
9255 Sunset Blvd.
Los Angeles, California 90069

L

A La Mode Music (ASCAP)
1236 Redondo Blvd.
Los Angeles, California 90019

La Rana (BMI)
1750 E. Holly Avenue
El Segundo, California 90245

Land of Music Publishing (ASCAP)
1136 Gateway Lane
Nashville, Tennessee 37220

Largo Music, Inc. (ASCAP)
425 Park Avenue
New York, New York 10022

Lars (ASCAP)
Address unknown

Lawyer's Daughter (BMI)
Homestead Road
Pottersville, New Jersey 07979

Lena May (ASCAP)
c/o SBK Songs
810 Seventh Avenue
New York, New York 10019

Leona (ASCAP)
Address unknown

Let There Be Music Inc. (ASCAP)
see Buzz Cason Publications Inc.

Levay (ASCAP)
see Giorgio Moroder Publishing Co.

Level 42 Songs (ASCAP)
Address unknown

Lido Music Inc. (BMI)
c/o Segel & Goldman Inc.
9348 Santa Monica Blvd.
Beverly Hills, California 90210

Lillybilly
see Bug Music

Lincoln Pond Music (BMI)
3888 Alta Mesa Drive
Studio City, California 91604

Dennis Linde Music (BMI)
35 Music Square E.
Nashville, Tennessee 37203

Little Doggies Productions Inc. (ASCAP)
(Stray Notes Music Division)
c/o Dennis Katz, Esq.
845 Third Avenue
New York, New York 10022

A Little More Music Inc. (ASCAP)
P.O. Box 120555
Nashville, Tennessee 37212

List of Publishers

Little Shop of Morgansongs (BMI)
1102 17th Avenue S.
Nashville, Tennessee 37212

Little Steven Music (ASCAP)
Address unknown

Little Tanya (ASCAP)
see MCA Music

Lodge Hall Music, Inc. (ASCAP)
12 Music Circle, S.
Nashville, Tennessee 37203

Lyle Lovett (ASCAP)
c/o Michael H. Goldsen Inc.
6124 Selma Avenue
Hollywood, California 90028

Lu Ella (ASCAP)
see WB Music Corp.

Lucky Break (ASCAP)
c/o Jimmy George
5461 Kester Avenue
Van Nuys, California 91401

Lucrative (BMI)
PO 90363
Nashville, Tennessee 37209

M

Makiki Publishing Co., Ltd. (ASCAP)
9350 Wilshire Blvd., Suite 323
Beverly Hills, California 90212

Mambadaddi (BMI)
5606 Bennett Avenue
Austin, Texas 78751

Marilor Music (ASCAP)
3970 Overland Avenue
Culver City, California 90230

Mick Mars (BMI)
9255 Sunset Blvd.
Los Angeles, California 90069

MCA, Inc. (ASCAP)
c/o Mr. John McKellen
445 Park Avenue
New York, New York 10022

MCA Music (ASCAP)
Division of MCA Inc.
445 Park Avenue
New York, New York 10022

Medicine Hat Music (ASCAP)
c/o Gelfand, Rennert & Feldman
Att: Babbie Green
1880 Century Park, E., No. 900
Los Angeles, California 90067

Megadude (ASCAP)
Address unknown

Meow Baby (ASCAP)
Address unknown

Midstar Music, Inc. (BMI)
1717 Section Road
Cincinnati, Ohio 45237

Midsummer Music (ASCAP)
see April Music, Inc.

Mietus Copyright Management (BMI)
P.O. Box 432
2351 Laurana Road
Union, New Jersey 07083

Mighty Nice Music (BMI)
12 Bash Place
Houston, Texas 77027

Mighty Three Music (BMI)
c/o Earl Shelton
309 S. Broad Street
Philadelphia, Pennsylvania 19107

Mijac Music (BMI)
c/o Warner Tamerlane
Publishing Corp.
900 Sunset Blvd., Penthouse
Los Angeles, California 90069

Missing Ball (BMI)
211 E. 57th Street
New York, New York 10022

Moolagenous (ASCAP)
see WB Music Corp.

Moon & Stars Music (BMI)
see Cotillion Music Inc.

Moonwindow Music (ASCAP)
c/o David Ellingson
737 Latimer Road
Santa Monica, California 90402

Mopage (BMI)
Address unknown

Morning Crew (BMI)
see Irving Music Inc.

Giorgio Moroder Publishing Co. (ASCAP)
Att: George Naschke
4162 Lankershim Blvd.
North Hollywood, California 91602

Gary Morris Music (ASCAP)
Att: Gary Morris
Rt. 3
Hunting Creek Road
Franklin, Tennessee 37064

Mother Bertha Music, Inc. (BMI)
c/o Phil Spector International Inc.
P.O. Box 69529
Los Angeles, California 90069

Motley Crue (BMI)
see WB Music Corp.

MPL Communications Inc. (ASCAP)
c/o Lee Eastman
39 W. 54th Street
New York, New York 10019

Muffin Stuffin (BMI)
3624 Fir
San Diego, California 92104

Music Corp. of America (BMI)
see MCA, Inc.

My My Music (ASCAP)
Address unavailable

N

NAH Music (ASCAP)
c/o Levine & Epstein
485 Madison Avenue
New York, New York 10022

Nero Publishing (ASCAP)
505 Jocelyn Hollow Court
Nashville, Tennessee 37205

New Hidden Valley Music Co. (ASCAP)
c/o Ernst & Whinney
1875 Century Park, E., No. 2200
Los Angeles, California 90067

New World Music Corp. (NY) (ASCAP)
75 Rockefeller Plaza
New York, New York 10020

Next o Ken (BMI)
Route 4, New Hwy. 96W
Franklin, Tennessee 37064

Night Garden Music (BMI)
c/o Unichappell Music, Inc.
810 Seventh Avenue, 32nd Fl.
New York, New York 10019

No Ko Music (ASCAP)
c/o Bug Music Group
6777 Hollywood Blvd., 9th Fl.
Hollywood, California 90028

No Pain, No Gain (ASCAP)
see MCA Music

Nonpariel Music (ASCAP)
see Walden Music, Inc.

November Nights (ASCAP)
see Chappell & Co., Inc.

Now & Future (ASCAP)
see Southern Music Publishing Co., Inc.

Now Sounds Music (BMI)
1880 Century Park, E., 9th Fl.
Los Angeles, California 90067

O

Of the Fire Music (ASCAP)
c/o Daniel Zanes
117 Pembroke Street
Boston, Massachusetts 02118

Off Backstreet Music (BMI)
90 Universal City Plaza
Universal City, California 91608

On the Move
Address unknown

OPC (ASCAP)
c/o Buttermilk Sky Assoc.
515 Madison Avenue, Suite 1717
New York, New York 10022

P

Pacific Island Music (BMI)
see Arista Music, Inc.

Martin Page (ASCAP)
c/o WB Music
9000 Sunset Blvd.
Los Angeles, California 90069

Pal-Park Music (ASCAP)
c/o Mitchell-Silberberg-Knupp
11377 W. Olympic Blvd., Suite 900
Los Angeles, California 90064

Pamalybo (BMI)
see Irving Music Inc.

Panchin (BMI)
c/o Alan N. Skiena
200 W. 57th Street
New York, New York 10019

Pardini
Address unknown

Patchwork Music (ASCAP)
c/o David Loggins
P.O. Box 120475
Nashville, Tennessee 37212

Paul & Jonathan (BMI)
Route 2, Box 129
Kingston Springs, Tennessee 37082

Paulanne Music Inc. (BMI)
c/o Feinman & Krasilovsky
Att: Andrew J. Feinman, Esq.
424 Madison Avenue
New York, New York 10017

Peer International Corp. (BMI)
see Peer-Southern Organization

Peer-Southern Organization
1740 Broadway
New York, New York 10019

Perceptive (ASCAP)
see Hideaway Hits

Piano (BMI)
c/o Connie Heigler
309 W. Broad Street
Philadelphia, Pennsylvania 19107

Pink Pig Music (BMI)
c/o Funky But Music
P.O. Box 1770
Hendersonville, Tennessee 37075

Polygram Music Publishing Inc. (ASCAP)
Att: Brian Kelleher
c/o Polygram Records Inc.
810 Seventh Avenue
New York, New York 10019

Polygram Songs (BMI)
810 Seventh Avenue
New York, New York 10019

Poopys (ASCAP)
see WB Music Corp.

Poperetta (BMI)
  c/o Delores Jabara
  12 Windy Hill Road
  Westport, Connecticut 06880

Elvis Presley Music, Inc. (BMI)
  c/o Chappell & Co.
  810 Seventh Avenue
  New York, New York 10019

Theodore Presser Co. (ASCAP)
  Presser Place
  Bryn Mawr, Pennsylvania 19010

Pretty Man (BMI)
  Address unknown

Prince Street Music (ASCAP)
  Att: John Frankenheimer, Esq.
  Loeb & Loeb
  10100 Santa Monica Blvd.
  Suite 2200
  Los Angeles, California 90046

Protoons Inc. (ASCAP)
  c/o Profile Records Inc.
  Att: Cory Robins
  740 Broadway, 7th Fl.
  New York, New York 10003

PSO Ltd. (ASCAP)
  see Peer-Southern Organization

Pub Pending 78 (ASCAP)
  see Theodore Presser Co.

Q

Quackenbush Music, Ltd. (ASCAP)
  c/o Gelfand, Rennert & Feldman
  Att: Babbie Green
  1880 Century Park, E., No. 900
  Los Angeles, California 90067

A Question of Material (ASCAP)
  Address unknown

R

Ransaca (ASCAP)
  Address unknown

Rare Blue Music, Inc. (ASCAP)
  645 Madison Avenue, 15th Fl.
  New York, New York 10022

Raski (ASCAP)
  see Ensign Music Corp.

Ready for the World Music (BMI)
  600 Renaissance Center
  Detroit, Michigan 48243

Realsongs (ASCAP)
  Address unknown

Regent Music (BMI)
  110 E. 59th Street
  New York, New York 10022

Reggatta Music, Ltd.
  c/o Phillips Gold & Co.
  1140 Avenue of the Americas
  New York, New York 10036

Revelation Music Publishing Corp.
  (ASCAP)
  Tommy Valando Publishing Group Inc.
  1270 Avenue of the Americas
  Suite 2110
  New York, New York 10020

Rightsong Music Inc. (BMI)
  see Chappell & Co., Inc.

Rilting Music Inc. (ASCAP)
  see Fiddleback Music Publishing Co.,
  Inc.

Riva Music Ltd. (ASCAP)
  see Arista Music, Inc.

River House (BMI)
  c/o Willie Nile
  257 Kenview Blvd.
  Buffalo, New York 14215

List of Publishers

Riverstone (ASCAP)
Address unknown

Robertson Publishing (ASCAP)
Address unknown

Rounder (ASCAP)
Address unknown

Roundhead (BMI)
1900 Avenue of the Stars
Los Angeles, California 90067

R.U. Cerious (ASCAP)
Address unknown

Rumble Seat (BMI)
c/o Randy Sharp
14321 Valerio Street
Van Nuys, California 91405

Rush Groove (ASCAP)
405 W. 45th Street
New York, New York 10036

Rutland Road (ASCAP)
see Almo Music Corp.

S

Carole Bayer Sager Music (BMI)
c/o Segel, Goldman & Macnow Inc.
9348 Santa Monica Blvd.
Beverly Hills, California 90210

Saja Music (BMI)
c/o Le Frak Ent.
40 W. 57th Street
New York, New York 10019

Scarlet Moon Music (BMI)
P.O. Box 120555
Nashville, Tennessee 37212

Don Schlitz Music (ASCAP)
P.O. Box 120594
Nashville, Tennessee 37212

Science Lab (ASCAP)
c/o SBK Songs
810 Seventh Avenue
New York, New York 10019

Scoop (ASCAP)
Address unknown

Screen Gems-EMI Music Inc. (BMI)
6255 Sunset Blvd., 12th Fl.
Hollywood, California 90028

Seabreeze (ASCAP)
see WB Music Corp.

Sharp Circle (ASCAP)
PO 121227
Nashville, Tennessee 37212

Sheddhouse Music (ASCAP)
27 Music Circle, E.
Nashville, Tennessee 37203

Shipwreck (BMI)
c/o Ellen Shipley
55 Third Place
Brooklyn, New York 11231

Short Order (ASCAP)
see MCA Music

Sikki Nixx (BMI)
9255 Sunset Blvd.
Los Angeles, California 90069

Silver Fiddle (ASCAP)
c/o Segel & Goldman Inc.
9200 Sunset Blvd., Suite 1000
Los Angeles, California 90069

Silverline Music, Inc. (BMI)
329 Rockland Road
Hendersonville, Tennessee 37075

Paul Simon Music (BMI)
1619 Broadway
New York, New York 10019

Singletree Music Co., Inc. (BMI)
815 18th Avenue, S.
Nashville, Tennessee 37213

Sister Fate Music (ASCAP)
c/o Cooper, Epstein & Hurewitz
9465 Wilshire Blvd.
Beverly Hills, California 90212

Skull Music (BMI)
c/o Mac Rebennack
1995 Broadway
New York, New York 10023

Skunk Deville (BMI)
General Delivery
Bexar, Arkansas 72515

Slick Fork Music (ASCAP)
see Bug Music

Snow Music
c/o Jess Morgan & Co., Inc.
6420 Wilshire Blvd., 19th Fl.
Los Angeles, California 90048

Snowden Music (ASCAP)
344 W. 12th Street
New York, New York 10014

Songs of Jennifer (ASCAP)
c/o Entertainment Music Co.
1700 Broadway, 41st Fl.
New York, New York 10019

Southern Music Publishing Co., Inc.
(ASCAP)
Att: Ralph Peer, II
1740 Broadway
New York, New York 10019

Southern Nights Music Co. (ASCAP)
35 Music Square, E.
Nashville, Tennessee 37203

Southwing (ASCAP)
1300 Division, Suite 202
Nashville, Tennessee 37203

Special Rider Music (ASCAP)
P.O. Box 860, Cooper Sta.
New York, New York 10276

Spoondevil (BMI)
see Bug Music

Bruce Springsteen Publishing (ASCAP)
c/o Jon Landau Management, Inc.
Att: Barbara Carr
136 E. 57th Street, No. 1202
New York, New York 10021

Sputnick Adventure (ASCAP)

Stazybo Music (BMI)
see Mietus Copyright Management

Billy Steinberg Music (ASCAP)
c/o Manatt, Phelps, Rothenberg &
Tunney
11355 W. Olympic Blvd.
Los Angeles, California 90064

Stranger Music Inc. (BMI)
c/o Machat & Kronfeld
1501 Broadway, 30th Fl.
New York, New York 10036

Stray Notes Music (ASCAP)
see Little Doggies Productions Inc.

Streamline Moderne (BMI)
see Off Backstreet Music

Stymie Music (ASCAP)
Address unknown

Su-Ma Publishing Co., Inc. (BMI)
P.O. Box 1125
Shreveport, Louisiana 71163

Sweet Angel Music (ASCAP)
c/o Michael H. Goldson, Esq.
6124 Selma Avenue
Hollywood, California 90028

Sweet Cyanide (BMI)
see Willesden Music, Inc.

List of Publishers

Swiftwater Music (ASCAP)
Att: David L. Frishberg
6053 Burralo Avenue
Van Nuys, California 91401

Swirling Vortex (ASCAP)
Address unknown

T

Talmont Music Co. (BMI)
c/o Pickwick International
1370 Avenue of the Americas
Suite 603
New York, New York 10019

Tapadero Music (BMI)
815 18th Avenue S.
Nashville, Tennessee 37203

TCF (ASCAP)
see WB Music Corp.

Tee Girl Music (BMI)
c/o Lipservices
263 West End Avenue
New York, New York 10023

Teete (BMI)
c/o Bob Lieberman
825 N. San Vicente
Los Angeles, California 91608

Terrace Music (ASCAP)
see Blue Lake Music

Texas City (BMI)
c/o Backstreet
90 Universal City
Universal City, California 91608

Threesome Music
1801 Avenue of the Stars, Suite 911
Los Angeles, California 90067

Timic (ASCAP)
Address unknown

George Tobin (BMI)
c/o Studio Sound
11337 Burbank Blvd.
North Hollywood, California 91601

Tomato du Plenti (ASCAP)
Address unknown

Tongerland (BMI)
see Bug Music

Tools (BMI)
c/o Jim Tullio
405 N. Wabash
Chicago, Illinois 60611

Townsway Music (BMI)
c/o Mr. Garry Kief
P.O. Box 69180
Hollywood, California 90069

Tree Publishing Co., Inc. (BMI)
P.O. Box 1273
Nashville, Tennessee 37203

Trio Music Co., Inc. (BMI)
1619 Broadway
New York, New York 10019

Triple Star (BMI)
1875 Century Park E.
Los Angeles, California 90067

Trixie Lou Music (BMI)
14234 Grandmont
Detroit, Michigan 48227

TRO-Hollis Music, Inc. (BMI)
10 Columbus Circle, Suite 1460
New York, New York 10019

Troph
Address unknown

Troutman's Music (BMI)
c/o Larry Troutman
2010 Salem Avenue
Dayton, Ohio 45406

TSP Music, Inc.
1875 Century Park, E., Suite 700
Los Angeles, California 90067

Two-Sons Music (ASCAP)
44 Music Square, W.
Nashville, Tennessee 37203

U

Ultrawave (ASCAP)

Uncle Artie (ASCAP)
Address unknown

Uncle Ronnie's Music Co., Inc. (ASCAP)
1775 Broadway
New York, New York 10019

Underdog (BMI)
PO 1517
Key Largo, Florida 33037

Unichappell Music Inc. (BMI)
810 Seventh Avenue, 32nd Fl.
New York, New York 10019

Unicity Music, Inc. (ASCAP)
c/o MCA Music
445 Park Avenue
New York, New York 10022

United Artists Music Co., Inc.
6753 Hollywood Blvd.
Los Angeles, California 90028

United Lion Music Inc. (BMI)
c/o United Artists Corp.
729 Seventh Avenue
New York, New York 10019

Upward Spiral
see WB Music Corp.

USA Exotica (ASCAP)
see WB Music Corp.

U2 (ASCAP)
see Chappell & Co., Inc.

V

Vabritmar (BMI)
15445 Ventura Blvd.
Sherman Oaks, California 91413

Virgin Music, Inc. (ASCAP)
Att: Ron Shoup
43 Perry Street
New York, New York 10014

Virgin Music Ltd. (ASCAP)
see Chappell & Co., Inc.

Virgin Nymph (BMI)
90 University Place
New York, New York 10003

Vogue Music (BMI)
see Welk Music Group

W

Waifersongs Ltd. (ASCAP)
c/o Michael C. Lesser, Esq.
225 Broadway, Suite 1915
New York, New York 10007

Walden Music, Inc. (ASCAP)
Att: Bonnie Blumenthal
75 Rockefeller Plaza
New York, New York 10019

Warlock Music (ASCAP)
see Island Music

Warner Brothers, Inc. (ASCAP)
9000 Sunset Blvd.
Los Angeles, California 90069

Warner-Elektra-Asylum Music Inc. (BMI)
1815 Division Street
Nashville, Tennessee 37203

Warner House of Music (BMI)
9000 Sunset Blvd., Penthouse
Los Angeles, California 90069

Warner-Refuge Music Inc. (ASCAP)
1815 Division Street
Nashville, Tennessee 37203

List of Publishers

Warner Springs (ASCAP)
see WB Music Corp.

Warner-Tamerlane Publishing Corp.
(BMI)
see WB Music Corp.

Wavemaker Music Inc. (ASCAP)
c/o Lipservices
263 West End Avenue
New York, New York 10023

WB Gold Music Corp. (ASCAP)
c/o Warner Brothers Music
9000 Sunset Blvd., Penthouse
Los Angeles, California 90069

WB Music Corp. (ASCAP)
c/o Warner Brothers, Inc.
Att: Leslie E. Bider
9000 Sunset Blvd., Penthouse
Los Angeles, California 90069

WBM (SESAC)
see Warner Brothers, Inc.

Web 4 Music Inc. (BMI)
2107 Faulkner Road, N.E.
Atlanta, Georgia 30324

Webo Girl Music/WB Music Corp.
(ASCAP)
c/o Rubin, Baum, Levin, Cowstant,
Friedman
645 Fifth Avenue
New York, New York 10022

Welbeck Music
see Cherry Lane Music Co., Inc.

Welk Music Group
1299 Ocean Avenue, Suite 800
Santa Monica, California 90401

Welsh Witch Publishing (BMI)
c/o Gelfand, Breslauer, Rennert &
Feldman
1880 Century Park, E., Suite 900
Los Angeles, California 90067

Maurice White (ASCAP)
Address unknown

Whitesnake (ASCAP)
Address unknown

Wild Gator Music (ASCAP)
see Gomace Music, Inc.

Will Music (ASCAP)
Address unknown

Willesden Music, Inc. (BMI)
c/o Zomba House
1348 Lexington Avenue
New York, New York 10028

William V (ASCAP)
see Welk Music Group

Willin' David (BMI)
1205 16th Avenue, S.
Nashville, Tennessee 37212

Wing & Wheel (BMI)
c/o Bug Music
6777 Hollywood Blvd.
Hollywood, California 90028

Wooden Wonder (SESAC)
Address unknown

Writer's Group Music (BMI)
P.O. Box 120555
Nashville, Tennessee 37212

Wyoming Flesh (ASCAP)
c/o Mitchell Froom
4720 W. First Street
Los Angeles, California 90004

Y

Yiggy (ASCAP)
see Irving Music Inc.

Yonder (ASCAP)
see WB Music Corp.

Young Millionaires Club (BMI)
see MCA Music

Z

Zappo Music (ASCAP)
Att: Bruce R. Hornsby
16815 Hartland Street
Van Nuys, California 91406

Zero Productions (BMI)
c/o Clog Holdings
3300 Warner Blvd.
Burbank, California 91501

Zevon Music Inc. (BMI)
c/o Jess Morgan & Co., Inc.
6420 Wilshire Blvd., 19th Fl.
Los Angeles, California 90048

Zomba Enterprises, Inc. (BMI)
c/o Zomba House
1348 Lexington Avenue
New York, New York 10128

Zookini (ASCAP)